Internships in Sport Management

by
Robin Ammon, Jr., EdD
Matthew Walker, PhD
Edward E. Seagle, EdD
Ralph W. Smith, PhD

Venture Publishing, Inc.
State College, PA

Production Manager: Richard Yocum
Manuscript Editing: George Lauer, Richard Yocum

Library of Congress Catalogue Card Number 2010940418
ISBN-10: 1-892132-91-5
ISBN-13: 978-1-892132-91-8

Internships in Sport Management

Table of Contents

Self-Confidence
Thinking Outside the Box
Strengths and Weaknesses
Professional Use of Technology
Summary

Internship/Career Direction
Internship Goals
Career Goals
Caution
Internship Timeline
Summary

Search
    Search Step #1: Identify Essential Characteristics of Agencies
    Search Step #2: Determine Your Own Needs and Preferences
    Search Step #3: Prioritize Your Needs and Preferences
    Search Step #4: Identify Resources for Information on Agencies
    Search Step #5: Compile a List of Potential Internship Agencies
    Search Step #6: Conduct an Informational Interview
Research
    The Internet
    University Files and Resources
    Telephone Calls
    Voice Mail
    Mail
    Internship (Job) Description
    Speak with Current or Past Interns at the Agency
    Volunteer at the Agency
Summary

Chapter One
Self-Assessment

The difference between a successful person and others is not a lack of strength, not a lack of knowledge, but rather a lack of will.

---VINCE LOMBARDI---

The ability to determine who you are and the attributes you have to offer a sport organization is paramount for your future success. Components of this self-determination include examining your self-confidence; establishing a personal "game plan for success"; identifying your interests, needs, and wants; recognizing your strengths and weaknesses; and assessing your ability to use technology. Investigating who you are becomes essential because your cumulative life experiences help to shape your decision-making process, which will impact your career choices. You need to remember that the ideal internship is one that leads to a full-time position. Therefore, understanding who you are and how you intend to pursue an internship becomes part of your "game plan for success." An important concept to remember is *proper planning prevents poor performance.*

Self-Confidence

Self-confidence is an absolute necessity for future success. Believing you can accomplish a task is half the battle. If you believe in yourself, you will become more self-confident, which causes others to believe in you as well. Michael Jordan once said, "Some people want it to happen, some wish it would happen, and others make it happen." You need to believe in yourself in order to make it happen! You are probably thinking to yourself, okay, so how do I "make it happen"? Actually, the process is not a difficult one. You need to identify positive and negative statements (i.e., internal messages) that you make to yourself. By identifying the negative thoughts, you can begin to work on them.

Ask yourself the following questions. If you answer in the affirmative, you can assist in *growing* your self-confidence, which as previously stated will enhance other people's belief in you as well. So here we go…

- Do you regularly acknowledge your positive accomplishments?
  - Examples include the following types of positive internal messages: *I did an excellent in-depth analysis for my Sport Law research paper. I established a timeline and kept to it, which allowed for multiple drafts. By not procrastinating I was able to submit the paper three days early. My grade reflected all the hard work I put into the paper. Way to go!*
- When approaching a difficult task, do you give yourself a pep talk to ensure a positive frame of mind?
  - Examples include: *I submitted a high-quality résumé and cover letter. I have researched the internship and have had my roommates ask me multiple questions that I may be asked during the interview. I have prepared myself to the best of my abilities and I know what it will take to succeed in this internship. My preparation and planning have prepared me to for this interview. I am confident in my abilities.*
- Have you practiced your oral communication skills?
  - Examples include: *Establish good eye contact. Use hand gestures and voice inflection to emphasize important points. Exude an aura of knowledge and confidence. Update yourself on the current industry terminology and be aware of any recent changes that could potentially impact the internship.*

Now, consider any types of actions or beliefs that may undercut your self-confidence. Ask yourself the following questions. Each "yes" answer may mean that you are impeding your chance to *grow* your self-confidence. Unfortunately, this may negatively impact others' belief in you as well.

- Do you criticize yourself for making mistakes or errors?
  - Examples include the following types of *negative* internal messages: *I can't believe I procrastinated again on that assignment in Sport Marketing! I didn't leave myself enough time to review the paper before submitting it. How could I be so stupid not to complete the assigned reading?*
- Do you sabotage your efforts with negative thoughts when approaching a difficult challenge? Examples include: *I don't have the necessary experience for this position. There are better qualified people for the internship. My interviewing skills suck.*
- Ignore or dilute your previous experiences?
  - Examples include: *If it weren't for Dr. Garcia, my résumé would be substandard. My girlfriend's father got me the internship, not me.*

Take some time during the next few weeks and analyze your thoughts. Are they constructive and therefore do they *positively* impact how you feel about yourself? Or are they *negative*, perpetuating your lack of belief in yourself? *You* are the only person who can control these thoughts. The process of eliminating these cynical attitudes is not easy. In most cases it is a marathon and not a sprint. It will take a great deal of perseverance and a lot of honesty on your part. Recognizing your pessimistic opinions and vowing to replace them with optimistic ones will lead to an increase in your self-confidence and ultimately maximize your results. Remember that nothing that is worthwhile in life comes easy.

We have provided some *Examples of Success* (below). In some cases these individuals faced insurmountable odds, but persistent self-confidence as well as a positive *attitude* helped them achieve a successful outcome.

Examples of Success

Review these examples of various individuals who successfully overcame challenges. Some of these individuals possess attributes we can only dream of, but others were normal individuals like you and me. Without self-confidence, their success would have been jeopardized.

- ▶ The people of New York City believing they could overcome the horrific events that took place on September 11, 2001.
- ▶ Nelson Mandela believing that after 27 years in prison, he could implement a multi-racial democracy ending South Africa's apartheid government's repressive regime.
- ▶ Brett Favre returning to the NFL at the age of 40, believing he could overcome the effects of old age and football naysayers who said he was washed up as a quarterback.
- ▶ Cal Ripken believing he could break Lou Gehrig's record by playing more than 2,130 consecutive Major League Baseball games.
- ▶ Michael Jordan, after retiring from a stellar career in the NBA to play Major League Baseball, returning to the Chicago Bulls to lead them to three NBA championships.
- ▶ Lance Armstrong, professional cyclist, believing he could successfully compete internationally after recovering from testicular cancer. He went on to become the only road-racing cyclist to win the prestigious Tour de France seven consecutive times.

Game Plan for Success

A *game plan for success* is something most people have not thought about. However, we challenge you to name a successful sport franchise or well-known corporation that does not possess such a plan. In business, these policies are termed "strategic plans," but they are similar in nature to a college athletic team's game plan for an upcoming opponent. How can you hope to complete a successful internship without understanding how it fits in your game plan? Possessing such a plan is important because it guides your efforts to succeed in the sport industry. A sound game plan for success allows you to determine where you want to go, similar to a road map. Of course, in this highly technological society, we just plug in our GPS system, but you get what we mean.

Hopefully by this point in your sport management career you have a distinct grasp of what constitutes sport management. The most important item to understand is that sport management pertains to the *business* of sport. It has *nothing* to do with coaching a sport, working with professional athletes, or being an athletic trainer. Unfortunately even after taking sport management courses for several years some students continue to see the word "sport" and don't see the word "management." Supervising the ticket office of a professional sport team, directing employees at a sport arena, coordinating compliance information for an intercollegiate athletic department, or managing the marketing efforts of an international motor sports event are examples of sport management positions. A major (or area of concentration) in sport management prepares students for careers in sport event management, intercollegiate athletic departments, minor league sport, sport facility management, sport marketing, sport promotions, and other areas of the expanding sport/business and sport/entertainment industries.

To determine your game plan for success it helps to look ahead to where you want to end up in sport. The type of position you hope to hold in sport business 5–10 years from now will be contingent on what you are doing in sport 3 years from now. The type of sport management position you have 3 years from now will depend on your position in sport 1 year from now. Finally, the type of sport management position you have a year from now is ultimately dependent on your internship. Do you now begin to understand the importance of that first step (internship) in your game plan for success? Once you have identified the direction you need to follow to meet your ultimate objective as a sport manager, you will be better able to answer fundamental questions about your professional future.

Application

At this point, complete Application 1.1.

Application 1.1: Devising Your Game Plan for Success

After writing a one-page narrative describing your game plan for success, you should be able to better understand where you want to be 5–10 years from now and the direction you need to pursue to accomplish that goal. Anything is possible if you make an attempt. As Wayne Gretzky was fond of saying, "you miss 100% of the shots that you don't take."

Overall Career Goal Statement

_____

_____

_____

_____

Area of Development	1-Year Goal	3-Year Goal	5–10-Year Goal
Area of Sport Industry			
Specific Job Title			
Duties/Responsibilities			
Salary Range			
Benefits			

Thinking Outside the Box

As W. Edwards Deming once said, "It is not necessary to change. Survival is not mandatory." If, however, you want to survive—and succeed—soon you will be required to make a very important decision… in what area of the sport industry you hope to land an internship as well as where in the country you want to complete an internship.

First of all, we need to discuss the difference between "wants" and "needs." For example, as a potential intern you must learn the difference between "wanting" a career and "needing" a job. *Careers* are long-term endeavors in a chosen field, but to be successful you need to have prepared yourself with the proper training and commitment to do whatever it takes to achieve that career. *Jobs* are temporary positions that individuals secure in order to pay the bills. Unfortunately, by not adequately preparing oneself, many individuals are relegated to a lifetime of "jobs" and they never achieve the "career" they envisioned as a sport management student. Some sport management students believe that all they need to do is finish their coursework, complete an internship, and a job in sport will magically appear. This will never happen. A career takes strategic planning (refer to your game plan for success), vision, sacrifice, and—every once in a while—the willingness to take a risk. However, not everyone possesses these attributes or they may not be willing to venture outside their comfort zone. If that is true for you… welcome to the world of jobs. You want a career? Keep reading!

Why are people stuck in the continuing "job" cycle? We believe there are three main reasons: Some students are what we term "geographically challenged." They don't understand that there are 49 states other than the one they reside in. Let's go back to what we were saying… if you want a career in sport, then you need to investigate where those careers are located. Some areas of the country possess higher levels of unemployment than others. Some students' frustration in not finding a career in sport is proportional to their stubbornness about leaving their local area.

As previously mentioned, the number of work-related opportunities in sport is extremely limited in some parts of the country. The competition for those careers that do exist is off the charts. Employers in the sport-industry (or any industry for that matter) want the "best" and the "brightest." So what type of sport-related jobs are available near where you live, as well as in most other parts of the country? Go to any online job summary database (such as TeamWork Online) and see what 90% of the positions involve. You guessed it… that five letter word that some students shudder to see… S-A-L-E-S. So what is so wrong with sales? Sales is nothing more than selling someone on the idea of purchasing a product. This is exactly what you try to do during an interview… correct? During an interview, the product is you and most of us have no problem in selling ourselves. Gaining experience in sales provides an unbelievably solid business foundation upon which "careers" are built. So do *not* whine about wanting a career in sport and then say, "but I don't want to sell." How does one avoid these previously mentioned problems? By looking "outside the box"… by being creative… by being a visionary. What are going to be the "hot" type of jobs in sport? Where can a smart student armed with a degree establish a niche? Here are several possibilities:

a) We believe positions working with sustainability ("going green") will be hot for the next 2-3 years.

b) Due to our aging population, anything to do with programming or fitness-related activities for seniors will be hot for the next 10 years.

c) There are over 2,500 universities and colleges in the United States. Most have some type of campus recreation program. Each of these programs needs to be managed in some capacity. Current students can acquire a wealth of experience by completing practicums/volunteer hours at a variety of nearby locations, including your campus recreation center.

d) Sport-related "service" providers will always have openings. Though they are a definite segment of the sport industry, these types of positions are not quite as attractive as others and therefore don't have the large number of applicants, but they usually pay fairly well. These types of careers include food and beverage companies, as well as companies that provide products for facilities and teams (stadium seating, lighting, and scoreboards, to name a few).

Again try not to limit yourself… expand the possibilities so you wake up with a *career* in sport and not a *job* hangover.

Strengths and Weaknesses

According to the North American Society for Sport Management (NASSM) website, there are over 300 undergraduate programs in the United States that provide some type of curriculum in sport management. Some universities have majors in sport management; others possess areas of concentration while the remaining consist of schools with focus areas. As a potential sport-management intern, you will be competing against students from these other programs. In addition, you may be competing against students who have previously completed an internship and believe they need a second or third one to secure the necessary experience to be hired. You will be competing against students from other majors like business or communications who desire a career in sport business. You will also be competing against students from graduate sport management programs. Folks, there is a *lot* of competition for an internship and later for a career in sport. So how will you differentiate yourself from these thousands of other individuals? You need to know your strengths and weaknesses, as well as your professional skills.

It is important for you to be aware of both your strengths and weaknesses. By knowing these qualities you will be able to highlight your strengths while concentrating on diminishing your weaknesses. In order to successfully secure an internship you must be able to *sell* yourself (remember how we discussed this previously) to the person who is interviewing you for the position. By knowing your strengths, you will be able to emphasize them during the application and interview process. Take some time to examine your skills and potential; this step will assist in your confidence about the "you" you are trying to sell.

At the same time you must also develop a specific plan for overcoming your limitations (weaknesses). During the weeks ahead, set goals that will help you eliminate or diminish these limitations. For example, if you often procrastinate on class assignments and group work, set reasonable goals for starting each project and a timeline for completion of the work (e.g., start the project at least 4 weeks prior and revisit it at least 1 hour per day). If you do not achieve your goal during the first phase, keep the goal the same and increase your determination to achieve it. If you *do* achieve your goal for the first week, raise your expectations for the next week, and so on. Establishing reasonable goals and working hard to achieve them can eliminate limitations. Reflect on what you are willing to commit to your internship agency. What specific things do you intend to do during your internship that will demonstrate your commitment to the organization, your interest in learning, and your dedication to the quality of your work? Make a list of the actions and behaviors that will demonstrate your *positive attitude* toward work and learning. This will notably include how many skills you intend to learn on the job and the number of hours you will work above and beyond the requirements from your college or university.

Applications 1.2–1.4 will assist you in identifying the skills or traits that you need to refine or acquire. As you begin your internship search, you must be mindful if any of these skills or traits are important for your success in that specific position. When completing these Applications, it is essential to be honest! Oftentimes, we are too close to ourselves to be impartial. A reliable strategy is to ask those who know us the best (family, friends, and roommates) to provide input. Sometimes these individuals seem to know us better than we know ourselves. It is also important that you take your time completing these Applications. If they are done in haste, you will not receive the maximum benefit from them. These Applications intend to help you know yourself, and knowing yourself well is the cornerstone to building a successful professional career.

Applications

Application 1.2 is a personal and professional assessment. List your past and present work experiences, plus any specific skills you acquired from each position. In addition, list any academic skills you gained in the classroom that you feel may prove pertinent for an internship in sport. After completing Application 1.2, continue on to Applications 1.3 and 1.4. These pertain to your professional skills as well as an assessment of your personality traits. Upon completing these checklists, you will become aware of your strengths and weakness, as well as any of traits and skills you possess that will be important for your success as a sport management intern.

Application 1.2: Personal and Professional Assessment

This Application is designed to assist you in examining your personal skills, achievements, and personality traits. Reflect on what professional and academic skills you have developed and what personality characteristics you demonstrate. Be honest and thorough in this self-evaluation. Use additional paper if needed.

PROFESSIONAL ASSESSMENT

Experience (Paid or Volunteer)   Skills acquired

_____

_____

_____

_____

_____

_____

_____

_____

EDUCATIONAL ASSESSMENT

What specific skills and knowledge have I gained from my sport management studies?

_____

_____

_____

_____

_____

_____

_____

_____

_____

Application 1.3: Professional Skills Assessment

The following professional skills may be paramount for an internship (or career) in the sport industry. This form may be used to identify specific professional skills you possess, plus those you need to refine or acquire. In addition, feel free to assess whether your skills match the requirements of the specific internship position you are seeking. This list is not comprehensive. Depending on the type of sport business position you are seeking, additional skills may be relevant. If so, feel free to add any additional professional skills that you want to assess.

Internship Position Title:				
Professional Skills	Already Possess	Already Possess But Need to Refine	Need to Acquire	Not Needed for Internship
Advising				
Analyzing				
Assessing				
Budgeting				
Communicating (written)				
Communicating (oral)				
Consulting				
Coordinating				
Decision Making				
Delegating				
Directing				
Evaluating				
Goal Setting				
Initiating				
Instructing				
Leading				
Managing				
Marketing				
Negotiating				
Organizing				
Planning				
Problem Solving				
Reporting				
Scheduling				
Selling				
Supervising				
Teaching				
Team Building				

Application 1.4: Your Top 10 Assets

Now that you have assessed the professional and personal skills that will help to make you successful, it is important to recognize that some of these skills are more important than others. You need to identify *your* most important assets (i.e., strengths), those that will ensure that you will be a "winner." Review the information you provided in Applications 1.2 and 1.3. Then, in the space provided below, identify your top 10 professional or personal assets.

1. _____

2. _____

3. _____

4. _____

5. _____

6. _____

7. _____

8. _____

9. _____

10. _____

Professional Use of Technology

The Internet, e-mail, social media, cell phones, and other technological innovations have dramatically changed the way people communicate with each other, both personally and professionally. Social networks (e.g., MySpace, Facebook, Twitter, and LinkedIn) for example, are popular ways for students (and professionals) to express themselves, as well as to connect with others. You should be aware, however, that many personnel departments and potential internship supervisors will check the Internet for information about an applicant. If you have placed unflattering or potentially embarrassing photos on the Internet or written a personal blog, you may lose the internship opportunity you are seeking. Before applying for an internship, be sure to review and "clean up" any unprofessional information contained on social networking sites. Anything that might call into question your moral or ethical character could drop you from an agency's interview list. You should also conduct a vanity search on your name using Google, to see if there is information about yourself on the Internet. You might be surprised at what you find.

We also suggest that you open an e-mail account that is used exclusively for internship-related correspondence. Be sure your e-mail address is professional. It sends the wrong message to a potential internship supervisor if your e-mail address is *cowboy-junkie-from-hell@yahoo.com* or *iloveshots@gmail.com*. You should also use professional language, not text message shorthand, when corresponding with a potential internship site supervisor via e-mail.

Summary

Chapter 1 provided you with the basics necessary to begin the process of securing a quality internship. The strategies we suggested will provide you with a "road map" to begin the process. While the information in this chapter presents a foundation, you must understand that you can't be successful without a game plan on how you intend to progress towards your goal of a career in sport business—*fail to plan; plan to fail!* Careers in the sport industry are extremely competitive; you need to be the best you can be and do whatever is necessary to be successful. Prospective employers are searching for sport management students with an unbelievable work ethic, extreme dedication, and a passion that will light up a room. Once you have mastered the information in this chapter, you can move ahead with confidence because you have created a sound cornerstone for your internship experience.

Chapter Two
Direction

Only those who will risk going too far can possibly find out how far one can go.

---T. S. ELIOT---

In Chapter 1 we discussed the importance of having a specific plan that will help you stay on the right track for a successful career in sport business. The well-known American humorist Will Rogers once said, "Even if you are on the right track, you'll get run over if you just sit there." This is true in sport management. Once you determine where you want to go, it is imperative to begin setting goals on how to get there. Setting goals is crucial because these goals provide the direction you need to make sound career-related decisions. This chapter will continue to provide you with a road map to a successful internship.

Internship/Career Direction

In Chapter 1 you established your game plan for success. You determined where you wanted to be in 5–10 years and then worked backwards to determine where you should concentrate your search for a related internship. Without knowing where you want to end up, you will have no idea which direction to take. In order to determine if you are going in the proper direction, you need to ask yourself a few basic questions that will help to clarify the ideal internship for you.

Application

Application 2.1 provides an opportunity for you as a prospective sport management intern to answer several critical questions pertaining to the direction you need to pursue during your internship. Your answers will assist in determining the proper direction you need to follow to fulfill your game plan for success. Identifying the correct route allows you to begin to contemplate the goals necessary to eventually secure the career you have previously identified.

Application 2.1: Establishing the Proper Direction

Part A. Questions

First of all, answer each question in the space provided below. Afterwards, go back and write down the direction (e.g., type of sport organization and specific practical work experience) you should take to pursue a successful internship that would lead to your previously identified career.

1. What practical experiences in sport management do I have to build upon?

Answer: _____

_____

_____

Direction: _____

_____

_____

2. At this point, what type of sport management experiences do I lack?

Answer: _____

_____

_____

Direction: _____

_____

_____

3. What type of work related to sport business do I enjoy most?

Answer: _____

_____

_____

Direction: _____

_____

_____

4. Ultimately, what kind of career in the sport industry do I want to have? (This will come from your completed game plan for success.)

Answer: _____

_____

_____

Direction: _____

_____

_____

5. What employment choices in sport business are viable for me upon graduation?

Answer: _____

_____

_____

Direction: _____

_____

_____

Part B. Internship and Career Direction

Examine your responses for questions 1–5. Based upon your answers and the direction you supplied, indicate the *ultimate direction* you think your internship and career should take. If you planned properly and gave your game plan for success a great deal of thought, your answer below should be similar. If not, review your game plan and determine why they are different.

_____

_____

_____

_____

_____

_____

_____

_____

Internship Goals

Let's discuss a couple of quick definitions. The term "university supervisor" will be used to describe the individual from your institution who is responsible for you meeting curriculum requirements established for your internship. We will call the internship location the "agency." The agency representative responsible for you during the internship will be called your "agency supervisor."

Now that you have identified your game plan for success, you have a career objective established in your mind. Every future experience related to sport needs to be related to that objective. This is when the road map, which we have previously mentioned, comes into play. Your road map will provide the direction you need to follow to successfully fulfill your game plan. Another term for direction is "goals." Setting clear and concise goals will ensure that you stay on the right track to meet your career objective. These goals not only need to be well thought out but they need to be communicated to your internship supervisor as well as your agency supervisor. By knowing and understanding the goals you have established to meet your career goals these individuals can assist you in fulfilling them. A word of caution: you will need to update constantly and tweak your goals to guarantee that you stay on course. Your goals are *not* static; they need to be flexible and you need to revisit them constantly.

Preparing these goals can be tricky. As we have previously discussed, in order to meet your 5–10-year game plan, you need to have both a 3-year and 1-year "checkpoint." You must view the internship as the springboard towards meeting your 1-year checkpoint. Your internship must be practical, in that it must provide the requisite experiences and skill acquisition that will adequately prepare you to meet your first checkpoint. Finally, the goals you set pertaining to your internship must be realistic; otherwise, you have wasted valuable time.

The preparation you carried out while establishing your game plan for success will identify what you want to learn (skills and knowledge) as well as *how* you want to learn them (experiences). The ideal internship will lead to a full-time employment offer, but this requires that you learn as much as possible during your internship. Once you have gained the requisite knowledge and skills, your work ethic needs to be of high enough caliber that you make yourself indispensible to your sport agency.

In order to identify the specific experiences and learning opportunities you hope to acquire during your internship, you must complete a thorough investigation about the various internship locations *before* accepting an internship. Developing a comprehensive list of goals that will guide your internship site selection is one strategy when conducting this research.

Writing Internship Goals

Goals are not as specific as objectives and are not necessarily observable and measurable. Therefore, when we speak of goals we are talking more along the lines of general outcome statements. They indicate what you expect to learn and experience during your internship. They must be specific enough to allow you and your supervisor to assess whether or not you are achieving your goals. However, as we mentioned, they also need to be flexible, since they will change as you increase your skill sets and acquire more knowledge specific to your area of interest. The following information will assist you in preparing an all-inclusive list of goals for your sport management internship.

1. Identify and include any generic skills important to a sport management practitioner. Leadership skills, interpersonal skills, and administrative skills are examples of generic skills.
2. Specify entry-level skills necessary for a student entering the sport industry. For example, the goals for someone interested in facility or event management goals may include planning, premise liability, and sponsorship acquisition, while a sport marketing student's goals might include skills related to marketing, accounting, and sales.
3. Build upon skills and practical experiences you already possess and identify skills that you need to obtain. Refer to Application 2.1, Questions 1 and 2, to help you.
4. Include action verbs whenever possible that spell out what you actually plan to do, rather than

focusing exclusively on what you want to learn. Though you may need some initial direction, in most cases you learn more by completing the activities yourself.

5. Make certain that you have been as comprehensive as possible when identifying the requisite goals. Review the information you have collected about the area of sport business in which you are interested. Only then can you compare your goals to the experiences the potential sport agency may offer.

6. Remember you are embarking on an internship for an entry-level position. Be realistic in your expectations. You are attempting to acquire the knowledge and skill sets that will prepare you for your first full-time position. Don't jump the gun and create goals for responsibilities you will take on 3 years from now. Refer back to your game plan.

Examples of Internship Goals

Carefully review the four internship goals we have provided. These are actual examples from sport management students who have volunteered to share their thoughts. Some of the goals are well written and some could use more detail. These goals will be appropriate for a variety of sport management internships, but remember your internship and career goals may be completely different. Be sure to use your own style and wording when writing *your* goal statements.

Internship Goals—Example #1

Ryan Walsh

During my internship, I would like to:

1. Implement and lead a successful adult recreation program.
2. Develop an emotional and influential video for the 2010 Help Us Help Others Campaign.
3. Establish an understanding of the YMCA Director position.
4. Have a positive influence on the lives of others.
5. Be a contributor to the continuing success of the facility.
6. Develop my leadership skills.
7. Increase the communication skills required to become an effective as well as efficient YMCA director.
8. Improve overall management skills.
9. Expand my network within the YMCA organization.

Internship Goals—Example #2

Jill Ponder

My internship goals are to:

1. Increase my network of industry professionals in order to ensure a successful career in broadcast journalism.
2. Become proficient in operating as well as maintaining all video-editing equipment in regards to sport broadcasting.
3. Assist with the setup of the television cameras and associated equipment for a Major League Baseball broadcast.
4. Achieve a thorough understanding of how a television set is run and operated for a major sports event.

5. Understand the importance of a strong work ethic and be able to withstand the number of hours required to broadcast a major sporting event.

6. Develop the initiative to accomplish the daily duties and responsibilities of the internship without being told by a supervisor.

7. Gain an appreciation of the communication skills necessary to effectively interact with a diverse staff.

8. Recognize the importance of effective time management skills and work to eliminate the temptation to procrastinate.

Internship Goals—Example #3

Eric Martin

My internship goals are to:

1. Learn day-to-day operations of a minor league baseball team, including but not limited to, stadium maintenance and inventory.

2. Increase the success rate in new season ticket sales.

3. Become skilled at general maintenance duties associated with being a stadium operator.

4. Demonstrate the ability to effectively market and sell season ticket plan renewals.

5. Learn the multiple aspects of game-day management, such as scheduling and staffing.

6. Gain firsthand customer service experience and ensure that everyone receives the best possible game experience.

7. Help organization set season stadium attendance record for third consecutive year.

8. Earn a job with the team or elsewhere in minor league baseball at the completion of my internship.

Internship Goals—Example #4

Courtney Cowen

My internship goals are to:

1. Gain insight into areas other than fan relations and promotions, such as finance, marketing, operations, and communications.

2. Continue networking and making contacts, especially with visiting teams, in order to have other potential options if I am unable to obtain a position from my internship.

3. Demonstrate a dedication and eagerness to learn by being the first one to arrive at the office and the last one to leave it.

4. Investigate what kind of green initiatives, if any, the organization is utilizing and then either implement or expand them as much as possible to help the organization be viewed as more socially responsible, as well as help the environment in Georgia and surrounding areas.

5. Expand the ability to take initiative and do things without being told, as well as be able to recognize what needs to be done, when it needs to be done, and how it needs to be done.

6. Discover more creative and innovative ways to improve the minor league organization and attract more fans.

7. Exhibit unmatched initiative by becoming more outgoing and providing input during staff meetings.

Application

Use the form provided in Application 2.2 to develop your own list of internship goal statements. A copy of your final list of goals will be given to both your university and agency supervisor and therefore needs to be reviewed multiple times to ensure that the wording makes sense and the sentences are grammatically correct.

Application 2.2: Internship Goals

Develop *at least* eight goals that you want to accomplish during your internship experience. Review the suggestions we made earlier in the chapter before you begin.

Goal #1: _____

_____

_____

Goal #2: _____

_____

_____

Goal #3: _____

_____

_____

Goal #4: _____

_____

_____

Goal #5: _____

_____

_____

Goal #6: _____

_____

_____

Goal #7: _____

_____

_____

Goal #8: _____

_____

_____

Career Goals

We have previously discussed your game plan for success, and you have determined your 3-year and 1-year "checkpoints" to ensure you are proceeding in the proper direction. You have also contemplated what type of internship will provide a good starting point for you to achieve your game plan. Then, after a great deal of thought and introspection, you created several internship goals. At this point it is important for you to appraise the work you have done so far. Do you see a definite connection between the goals you wish to accomplish during your internship, the internship you hope to secure, and your 1-year "checkpoint"? If not, you need to reassess your plan. Your game plan needs to be flexible, so don't be afraid to tweak it as necessary to make certain you are on the right track. Refer to our road map analogy. If you begin your trip on the wrong road, you won't be able to arrive at your intended destination.

Application

Application 2.3 provides a form to help you to review your game plan for success.

Application 2.3: Review Your Game Plan for Success

Use this form to make sure your career goals are consistent with your career direction information in Application 2.1. If they aren't, you may need to tweak your plan. Remember you need to have a connection between what you wish to accomplish during your internship, the internship you hope to secure, and your 1-year "checkpoint."

_____

_____

_____

_____

_____

_____

_____

_____

_____

_____

_____

_____

_____

_____

Caution

Completing coursework does *not* guarantee anyone will obtain an internship. Internship agencies and organizations are in the sport industry, and their bottom line in most instances is to show a profit. In order to secure a *meaningful* internship you, as a prospective intern, should possess all of the following. If you find you are experiencing problems securing an internship, you are probably deficient in one of these areas.

a. Working knowledge of computer software programs including Word, Excel, PowerPoint and desktop publishing

b. An understanding of *basic* finance, economics, budgeting, and accounting

c. The ability to communicate proficiently through verbal, written, and technological means

d. An awareness of how management, marketing, and sales techniques are utilized in the sport industry

e. Various practical experiences before the internship that make you appealing and marketable as an internship candidate

f. A *thorough* understanding of the host organization

g. An ability to value self-enhancement, self-concept, and self-actualization (These will be evident to prospective employers through your continued professional development, demonstrated by actions such as attending professional conferences related to the area of the sport you are interested and having memberships in related professional organizations)

h. An openness to new ideas and techniques

Internship Timeline

Now you need to evaluate what you need to accomplish before your internship. A variety of tasks and responsibilities are still ahead of you. In order to stay on task, you need to be organized and utilize proper time-management skills. The best way to do this is by use of an internship timeline. An effective timeline (similar to constructing an effective game plan for success) requires a great deal of thought and knowledge of where you hope to end up. The following suggestions will assist you in devising your timeline:

1. Identify all internship-related tasks you need to do between now and when you start your internship. This will require you to discuss the process with your university internship supervisor in addition to your academic advisor.

2. Organize the identified tasks chronologically, beginning with some of the applications we have already completed and progressing through to the start of your internship.

3. To effectively establish your deadlines, use a similar technique to the one you utilized in creating your game plan. Begin with the end result (your internship) and work backwards. Be smart and recognize that oftentimes some of us tend to procrastinate. You can help yourself overcome this problem by not only establishing "starting dates" but "target dates" for finishing each task as well. Finally put down a "completion date." Realize that some tasks will take longer than others. For example, remember that individuals who work for sport agencies have multiple tasks and responsibilities, and don't assume that returning your phone call or letter is a high priority for them. Their other duties, possible vacations, and being out sick may delay them in returning your correspondence.

4. It is important to stay on schedule; however you also must remain flexible with many of your target dates. You need to be prepared for some setbacks and to avoid panicking if you miss a target date or two. Unfortunately some dates are *not* flexible. These may include notifying your university internship supervisor (or Department Chair) about your intent to secure an internship. In addition, the deadline for notifying someone about the semester you intend to complete your internship may be inflexible as well.

Application

The following example provides a sample timeline with starting and target dates. Review this example and then construct one of your own in Application 2.4.

Sample Internship TimeLine

Task	Starting Date		Target Date		Completion Date
1. Develop your game plan for success and your related internship goals.	Jan.	18	Jan.	22	_____
2. Based on your *plan* compile a list of relevant internship sites.	Jan.	23	Jan.	25	_____
3. Discuss these potential agencies with appropriate faculty.	Jan.	26	Jan.	29	_____
4. Research information on potential agencies.	Jan.	30	Feb.	6	_____
5. Decide which agencies to pursue.	Feb.	7	Feb.	9	_____
6. Construct your résumé.	Feb.	9	Feb.	12	_____
7. Review résumé with appropriate faculty.	Feb.	15	Feb.	17	_____
8. Prepare your cover letter.	Feb.	15	Feb.	17	_____
9. Revise cover letter and résumé.	Feb.	18	Feb.	19	_____
10. Mail cover letters and résumés to selected agencies.	Feb.	19	Feb.	20	_____
11. Make follow-up phone calls to establish interview dates.	Mar.	1	Mar.	5	_____
12. Interview with relevant agencies.	Mar.	8	Mar.	19	_____
13. Send thank-you letter to interviewers.	Mar.	22	Mar.	26	_____
14. Select internship site.	Mar.	29	Mar.	31	_____
16. Register for internship credits at university.	Apr.	5	Apr	9	_____
17. Discuss selection with appropriate faculty.	Apr.	5	Apr.	9	_____
18. Confirm arrangements with internship supervisor (starting date, housing).	Apr.	12	Apr.	16	_____
19. Class finals.	May	3	May	7	_____
20. Travel home and collect requisite items.	May	10	May	14	_____
21. Travel to internship site and move into apartment.	May	17	May	21	_____
22. Begin internship.	May	24	May	24	_____

Students who plan to graduate at the end of their internship may want to add graduation-related deadlines to their timeline.

Application 2.4: Internship Timeline

Task	Starting Date	Target Date	Completion Date

Summary

For the majority of sport management students, a quality internship is the capstone experience. A lot of hard work, in-depth preparation, and a great deal of thought goes into planning for an internship. The amount of planning and preparation that takes place before the internship is oftentimes directly proportional to the quality of the internship experience. As Theodore Isaac Rubin once said, "Happiness does not come from doing easy work but from the afterglow of satisfaction that comes after the achievement of a difficult task that demanded our best."

This chapter helped you to develop a clear picture of what you want to achieve from your internship. Now it is time to explore how best to achieve these goals. The search process described in Chapter 3 will give you concrete examples of how to begin identifying agencies that will enable you to meet your internship goals.

Chapter Three
Search and Research

Success is not final. Failure is not fatal. It is the courage to continue that counts.

---Winston Churchill---

So far you have accomplished several of the *preliminary* steps necessary for finding an internship. In this chapter you will actually begin putting into practice everything you accomplished in chapters 1 and 2. Think of your imminent sport business career as building a house. Up to this point, you have gone through multiple planning stages (including your game plan for success). These would be similar to deciding the basic design of the house and associated structural decisions. In this chapter, you will select the location where the house will be built and begin delving into some of the specifics of the house such as type of exterior, color scheme and types of paint. Everything up to this point has just been part of the preparation process… now your actions will *really* begin to count!

   Searching for the right internship can be an arduous task, but successfully completing a game plan for success will assist to reduce the stress and anxiety. Remember that "nothing in life that is worthwhile comes easy." You must decide what is important and then attack that goal with an unbelievable fervor. Don't let anyone tell you that your goals are unachievable. The only difference between mediocrity and excellence is a little determination.

Search

Similar to building a house as you begin to consider various internship sites, you must decide what is important to you. In selecting a location for a house, factors such as proximity to schools or shopping centers, size of town, whether an urban or rural location, on a hill, in a valley, or close to a stream, and acreage all become important to you. The same is true for an internship. You need to decide your priorities and then determine what types of internships will meet your needs. Having determined your game plan already has mapped out where you want to end up in the sport industry. Now you need to find a location that will help you get there. As the saying goes, "keep your eyes on the prize." Remain focused on where you want to go.

   Before we get too far into the "search" discussion we need to mention an important concept that you mustn't ignore. You are looking for a *quality* internship. You want an internship that will provide valuable experience while allowing you the opportunity to make mistakes (or as we like to call them "learning experiences"). These learning experiences will provide you with know-how that you will be able to rely upon later in your career. In addition, you want to find an agency supervisor who will take the time to serve as your *mentor*. In other words, they will "teach you the basics" about the position. This individual believes they have a professional duty to ensure that you acquire all the knowledge and experience that will help with your professional success. They take pride in guiding you through the learning process involved with your internship, whether it be attending meetings, creating budgets, sitting on hiring committees, or just talking about the challenges you will face in your career. In addition, you want the opportunity to potentially be hired by the organization where you intern. Or if there are no available positions you want your agency supervisor to be willing to pick up the phone and call someone on your behalf. You do *not* want to secure an internship that is going to throw you into the job with little training and no guidance. Unfortunately, in a lot of situations sport agencies have realized they can decrease payroll expenses by rotating unpaid interns. They will start an intern in August, use him or her until the internship period is complete and then bring on another intern, never intending to hire any of them, no matter how good of a job they do. Therefore, you are in search of a *quality* internship that will result in preparing you for a "career" and not an organization that is just looking for a body to do a "job."

Student Perspective

The authors are well-known experts in the fields of sport management and recreation. We have accumulated over a hundred years of experience in these fields and will provide you with scores of strategies and techniques to ensure your successful journey in securing an internship in the business of sport. However, we must defer to an even more qualified group of individuals. These individuals are sport management alumni who have successfully navigated a major in sport management, completed an internship, and are now effectively employed in the sport industry. At various points during this text, we will include some of their comments. The following statements are some of the concerns they had as they began their search for a sport management internship.

1. Am I willing to re-locate to anywhere that will provide the most opportunity?

2. If hired to this organization, am I comfortable with a salary or position that may be slightly less than my ultimate expectation in order to gain a foot in the door?

3. What part of the country do I want to end up working in when I graduate? Then that's where my internship should probably be.

4. I need to get actual experience to make myself more marketable. Being just a grunt worker isn't worth my time or effort.

5. Money cannot dictate my decision.

6. Am I good enough to get an internship?

7. Am I qualified for any of these positions that are being offered?

8. Is my résumé/cover letter good enough to get an interview/internship?

9. What kind of things will I be doing during my internship?

10. For anyone going through the internship process for the first time, I would suggest starting your search early and making connections with prospective internship sites even earlier. Start by listing businesses where you are most interested in working as soon as you know that you will have to complete an internship. Then, write letters or emails to specific people (not "To Whom It May Concern") within those businesses to ask if they offer internships. You may be able to strengthen your connection by offering to volunteer in advance with any upcoming projects that the company could use extra help to complete. Showing initiative from the beginning will help you distance yourself from the countless other students that are requesting internships with generic bulk emails.

Thanks to Jason Hannold, Jakub Jaroszewicz, Mark Rhodehamel, and Brian Thompson.

Search Step #1: Identify Essential Characteristics of Agencies

As we previously mentioned, you should begin your search process by (1) determining the type of agency or organization that will meet your professional aspirations (when in doubt consult your *game plan*), and (2) determine where in the country these types of agencies are located.

As we stated in Chapter 1, unfortunately some students are "geographically challenged." They have determined that staying close to home and close to their family and friends is more important. Regrettably, unless you live in a large metropolitan area, the type of internship that will best provide the requisite practical experience to meet your 1- and 3-year goals may not be nearby. There are a total of 50 states in the United States, and the location that may be best suited to meet your game plan could be in any one of them (personally, we are partial to Hawaii). In addition, many international internship opportunities exist.

Undoubtedly, finances sometimes impact a student's decision where to secure an internship. This is understandable and, unfortunately, the number of paid internships has decreased exponentially. However, don't let the matter of several thousand dollars deter you from the internship that will best prepare you for a sport business career. Yes, an extra semester worth of financial aid or even a bank loan will mean additional payments; however, the benefits will most times outweigh the cost. Don't end up ten years from now lamenting a decision you made today. To repeat what we have been emphasizing throughout the first part of this text: careers in sport business are extremely competitive and if you want a career in sport then you need to investigate where those careers are located. If you don't, we can guarantee you that one of your competitors will!

Categories of Sport Organizations

By and large, your game plan for success will identify where in the sport industry you hope to establish a career. Intercollegiate or interscholastic athletic administration, sport marketing, sales, sponsorship acquisition, professional sports, facility or event management, non-profit sport (YMCAs), minor league sports, service organizations, concessionaires, and golf course or ski area management are but several of the many opportunities to choose from. Some of these, such as "sales," are fairly generic and can be combined with other areas. For example, you could work selling season-ticket packages for a Major League Baseball team. Or you could work selling scoreboards to athletic teams. Oftentimes these types of "generic" opportunities require minimal experience before a person might be hired full-time. In some of the more specialized areas of sport management, such as event management, it may take a great deal of experience before landing the first full-time position. An individual interested in this type of career may need to complete multiple internships before acquiring the level of experience necessary to be hired. Finally, you might be interested in facility operations. You could work in a facility, such as Heinz Field, that is one-dimensional and only hosts very specific types of events. Or you could work in facility operations for a multi-use facility, such as the Staples Center, that hosts a plethora of events such as basketball games, ice skating competitions, Monster Truck rallies, and concerts. Your goals will dictate the category of sport organization you select.

Search Step #2: Determine Your Own Needs and Preferences

This stage of the search process focuses upon identifying and prioritizing (1) professionally related internship needs and preferences and (2) personal internship needs and preferences. You should identify as many needs and preferences as possible.

Professionally Related Needs and Preferences

The first two chapters of this manual, as well as your game plan, helped you to identify your own personal and professional strengths and weaknesses as well as your career direction and interests. Now this information will be helpful in determining your own internship needs and preferences. Review chapters 1 and 2 and assess each of the Applications that you completed. In addition to analyzing these Applications, the following questions need to be answered regarding your professionally related needs and preferences.

Application

By completing the Professionally Related Needs and Preferences Form (Application 3.1), you will help to clarify some specific needs and preferences that your internship should provide.

Application 3.1: Professionally Related Needs and Preferences Form

The following list of questions will help you to identify factors to consider when selecting potential internship agencies. The identification of your professional needs and preferences is one variable to consider when determining the best sport business internship site. Circle "yes" or "no" for each of the following questions.

1. Is the size of the sport agency important to my career goals?　　Yes　　No
   If yes, what size agency am I seeking?

2. Do I want experiences in a specific specialization in sport business?　　Yes　　No
   If yes, what specialization?

3. Do I want to work with a specific level of sport (i.e., intercollegiate,　　Yes　　No
   interscholastic, minor league, or major league)?
   If yes, what level of sport?

4. Do I want a site where I hope to be hired full-time?　　Yes　　No

5. Should my internship provide opportunities different from my　　Yes　　No
   past experience?

6. Am I interested in a position where I will be closely supervised?　　Yes　　No

7. Do I prefer a specific geographic location for my internship?　　Yes　　No
   If yes, what specific region, state, or city?

List any additional professionally related needs or preferences.

_____

_____

_____

_____

_____

_____

_____

_____

_____

Personal Needs and Preferences

In addition to professional needs, each of you will have some personal needs that need to be taken into consideration as you begin your search. While your game plan for success identified the career in sport business you wish to attain, there are additional personal considerations that must be taken into account when determining your sport business internship location.

Application

The Personal Needs and Preferences Form (Application 3.2) asks specific questions related to your personal needs and preferences.

Application 3.2: Personal Needs and Preferences Form

Identifying personal needs and preferences is a second variable to consider when determining the best sport business internship location. Circle "yes" or "no" for each of the following questions.

1. Do I need financial or other assistance during my internship?   Yes   No

2. Do I need assistance in finding housing?   Yes   No

3. Do I need the ability to work part-time to earn additional money during my internship?   Yes   No

4. Will I have my own transportation while completing my internship?   Yes   No

5. Do I need to be near specific family or friends during my internship? If so, specify who they are and where they live.   Yes   No

List any additional personal needs or preferences.

_____

_____

_____

_____

_____

Search Step #3: Prioritize Your Needs and Preferences

The selection of your internship site is one of the most important decisions of your academic career. Therefore it is imperative to remember why you are considering a specific sport business internship location. The two previous application exercises identified your professional as well as personal needs and preferences for a sport business internship. Undoubtedly, some of these needs and preferences are more important than others. These priorities will often determine what direction your professional career takes. Consequently you should place particular emphasis on your *professionally* related needs and preferences. Since the priority of these needs and preferences will impact your overall decision, don't let a *preference* override a *need*.

Application

Keep in mind that the selection of your sport business internship is the first step in your game plan for success. Your professional and personal needs and preferences are important in the selection of a sport business internship site.

Application 3.3: Internship Selection Priority Form

Review Applications 3.1 and 3.2. Identify all "yes" responses, plus those that you added at the end of each form. After identifying these specific responses and your additions from Applications 3.1 and 3.2, use the Internship Selection Priority Form (Application 3.3) to list the 8 to 10 needs and preferences that are most important in your selection of a sport business internship site.

Then list the second most important criterion (either professionally related or personal).

Essential Criteria

Type of agency or organization (include any sport business specialization): _____

_____

_____

_____

Geographic location (if necessary):

_____

_____

_____

Needs and Preferences

Priority #1: _____

_____

_____

Priority #2: _____

_____

_____

Priority #3: _____

_____

_____

Priority #4: _____

_____

_____

Priority #5: _____

_____

_____

Priority #6: _____

_____

_____

Priority #7: _____

_____

_____

Priority #8: _____

_____

_____

Priority #9: _____

_____

_____

Priority #10: _____

_____

_____

Search Step #4: Identify Resources for Information on Agencies

As was previously mentioned, the quality of your internship will be directly proportional to the amount of work you invest. Just because you successfully complete your coursework, do not make the mistake that sport agencies are going to line up offering you the internship of your dreams. Make no mistake—today's economy and the thousands of other students interested in the same internships have made the process an extremely competitive one. There are a multitude of resources at your disposal to find an internship. The first three mentioned below are far and away the most important, while the others certainly can be utilized.

Networking

Networking, networking, networking! We emphasize this mantra to our students from the first day of their freshmen year. Ladies and gentlemen, the sooner you learn that it is not *what* you know, but *who* you know, the more successful you will be in the business of sport. *Nothing* in sport management is more important than your personal network. Networking is the ability to build alliances with multiple individuals in a variety of businesses. You notice that we didn't narrow it to just *sport* business. You never know which contact or person you meet will be the key that unlocks the door to your career in sport. *Anyone* you speak with could be a lead to the sport internship you desire. You remember our house-building analogy? The members of your network are a type of "tool" you can use to "build" your career. You want them to be able to work for you to identify possible job openings or to pick up the phone and call one of their contacts to recommend you for a position.

So, who makes up your initial network? In most cases, it is your family and friends you have known for years. Tell your family and friends that you are looking for an internship in the sport industry, and you'll be amazed at who knows whom. The second group in your network is your classmates. Professors who teach your classes and the alumni from your program are additional connections you need to cultivate for your network. If you have a desire to work in a particular field, chances are your sport management program has an alumnus currently working there. Ask your professors if they know of anyone who would be a good contact to get your foot in the door.

A word of caution: your network contacts are only valuable if they are *current*. You must stay in touch with members of your network to ensure they are an effective tool you can use to secure an internship or later on a position in sport business. Pick up the phone, send a brief email, text or tweet them, or even go "old school" and mail them a card. There are multiple methods at your disposal to ensure they know what you are doing and to keep you fresh on their mind. Your network needs to know your interests as well as your current status in order to efficiently work for you.

Every person you interact with is a contact and a potential lead. Learning how to develop and nurture a professional network will benefit you throughout your professional career. Don't be afraid to use those networks. Anyone who has previously walked in your shoes knows exactly how the game works.

Relatives/Friends

As we already discussed your family and friends are a great resource for both internships and full-time positions. It is amazing the number of times that Aunt Molly or Mr. Barnes at the end of the block either work in sport business or know someone who does. As mentioned earlier… *anyone* you meet may be an asset. However, in order to tap into these markets you need to have taken the time to speak with these individuals. These individuals can't help if they don't know of your interest. As the overused (but often relevant) saying goes, *think outside the box.* Does your college roommate's father work for a large sport marketing firm? Does your mom's sorority sister manage a fitness center? Is your uncle in charge of player personnel for the Minnesota Vikings? Each of these is an actual example from some of our students' experiences.

Faculty

As previously mentioned, it is vital to include your professors in your network. However, do not ignore the fact that these individuals have their own networks. Your sport management professors have been in the field for a number of years and undoubtedly know a variety of individuals in the sport industry. You want to be able to tap into these opportunities as well. Similar to every member in your network, your professors need to be up-to-date about your professional aspirations. Before they allow you access to their contacts, you need to have invested time in getting to know them. The more comfortable they feel and the more trust you have built with them, the better the chance you have of being permitted access to their professional network.

Practitioners

Practitioners in the sport industry are an excellent resource, especially if they are alumni of your college or university. These individuals should be included in your personal network. Make an attempt to establish a relationship with individuals in your area of interest as early as possible in your career. A good practice utilized by some sport management programs is to require their freshmen to interview an alumnus, or a practitioner, in a potential area of interest. Another excellent strategy is to volunteer with one of these individuals. Rarely will someone turn down "free" assistance. This "mini" internship (also called a practicum) will not only help you learn more about a specific area of sport business, but will also establish a relationship that potentially could assist with your internship or future employment opportunities.

The Internet

As a student growing up in the 21st century, you do not need to be told the value of the Internet. Ironically, in many situations you may be savvier with the Internet than those individuals you will intern with! If you haven't had the opportunity to develop an extensive personal network, if your sport management program is new or small, or if the individuals teaching in your program don't possess a background in sport management, the Internet can assist in identifying internship opportunities. The Internet also allows you to unearth contact information about sport agencies that may otherwise prove difficult to acquire.

Professional Organizations

Membership in a professional organization will not only provide you with contacts and increase your network, but also it will exhibit a commitment that looks good on your résumé. These memberships assist with your professional development and demonstrate your interest to other professionals in the field. Examples of these sport management organizations that you should consider joining include the North American Society for Sport Management (NASSM), Sport Marketing Association (SMA), Sport and Recreation Law Association (SRLA), Stadium Managers Association (SMA), Sporting Goods Manufacturing Association (SGMA), and the International Association of Assembly Managers (IAAM). Involvement now may not only help you find an internship, but may also assist you in finding employment in the field after graduation.

Conferences

Researching internship opportunities, establishing professional relationships, and expanding your network are multiple benefits that conferences afford students. Conferences also give a prospective intern the chance to learn more about a specific phase of sport business. Within the past several years, some conferences have evolved to where they cater specifically to sport management students. The Sport Entertainment and Venues Tomorrow (SEVT) conference held in Columbia, South Carolina, each November and the Georgia Southern Sport Management Conference held in Savannah, Georgia, each February are two such examples. Both of these conferences offer job fairs that present valuable information about internships and employment in sport business. In addition, the Georgia Southern Conference allows sport industry representatives the chance to recruit both interns and entry-level employees. These conferences attract the best students from throughout the country who are dedicated to finding careers in the sport industry.

Other industry conferences, such as the Stadium Managers Association conference, provide break-out sessions that permit students the chance to question practitioners about their duties and responsibilities. If you decide to attend one of these opportunities, be sure to bring multiple copies of your résumé and create a business card. Exchanging business cards is a tradition business professionals all over the world have utilized for decades. When you speak to a sport business professional, always ask for their business card. Having created your own business card to present to these individuals is not only a professional touch but will help to emphasize your level of interest. In addition, securing business cards from a variety of sources is an easy method to acquire contact information.

Sport Management Journals

Most sport management journals are research-oriented and therefore do not contain any internship information. Some trade organizations still print a magazine or journal but in today's turbulent economy, these are decreasing in numbers. Those organizations that still publish a journal now most often do so using the Internet to save publishing costs. Although magazines and journals do not generally carry ads for internships, they can help you become aware of opportunities, identify key professionals, and target innovative programs within the sport industry. When reviewing any magazine or journal, look at all aspects of the document including articles, advertisements, and promotions.

Internship or Job Announcements

Currently an overwhelming number of internship and job announcements are emailed by sport agencies as attachments to internship coordinators. In many cases, these are distributed by organizations that have a long-standing relationship with the internship supervisor. Depending on the reputation and industry connections that your internship coordinator possesses, these announcements can be a tremendous resource. If the organization has hosted a previous intern from your institution, they will contact your internship supervisor before they send the announcement out to other multiple sources. This is an example of the value of your internship coordinator's personal network. Unfortunately, as we discussed at the beginning of this chapter, in many cases organizations will utilize the "shotgun" approach and send out hundreds of announcements hoping the volume will entice enough candidates to apply. This is the tactic used by those agencies looking for a "body." Therefore, it becomes vital that you review announcements very carefully. Go over the entire announcement carefully. Once you have determined the announcement pertains to a *quality* internship, identify its key points. This will provide you with an understanding as to what the potential internship supervisor is looking for in an applicant and will give you an edge over other applicants because you are prepared.

Placement and Internship Centers

Most colleges and universities have job placement centers. Some may also have centers that focus exclusively on internships. Become acquainted with these offices and their staff members early in your college career. Placement and internship offices can provide assistance in a multitude of ways. For example, they can provide assistance in locating resource directories and writing cover letters and résumés. They may also set up practice interviews, give information on professional grooming skills, and offer other strategies regarding internships and employment. You must realize that, in most cases, they may not know anything about the sport business world and some of its unique nuances. However, we will cover most of these differences in this manual.

Libraries

Most university and college libraries possess a variety of specific resources, such as reference books, sport directories, and sport journals, that possibly may contain pertinent information about internships and employment. Though most of this information can now be obtained on the Internet, reference librarians are experts in helping to find specific resources.

Newsletters

Some sport business organizations still publish newsletters, but the majority of these newsletters are now on the Internet. Some of these newsletters contain job listings and internship information, but most of these organizations currently place this information on their web site. Those organizations that still publish newsletters generally distribute them to members only. If you become a member you have access to these publications. If you are not a member, contact one of your faculty members to see if they are a member. If so, you will still be able to access any pertinent information.

Search Step #5: Compile a List of Potential Internship Agencies

Previously in this chapter, in steps #1 & 2, you identified your professional and personal needs and preferences. Then in step #3, you prioritized those needs and preferences. Step #4 provided you with a number of potential resources you can use to search for your internship. Now we want you to use those resources and—keeping your priorities in mind—select 8–10 internship sites. As you go through this stage, be certain to keep your game plan in mind. Your plan must always guide the direction you intend to pursue, and therefore it should assist you as you begin to narrow your search. In addition, remember the discussion we had at the beginning of this chapter. You want a *quality* internship that will prepare you adequately. Focusing on your game plan and the fact that you are searching for a quality internship will help to eliminate multiple problems that many prospective interns face.

Search Step #6: Conduct an Informational Interview

As was mentioned in Chapter 1, proper planning prevents poor performance. In our situation, this statement means that as your internship search progresses, the planning and preparation you invest will influence the outcome. You need to become knowledgeable in every area that pertains to securing an internship. Therefore, as you begin to research your internship, let's consider some strategies you can use to your benefit.

Application

Contact your internship coordinator and ask for the name of an agency supervisor whom you could interview. It is important that this person has supervised interns in the past. You want someone with some experience under their belt. If your internship coordinator is unable to help, consider asking an alumnus of the program for a suggestion or, as a final option, contact one of the internship sites that did not make your top 10 list. It is better to not select an internship site where you plan to interview. Call the individual and ask if you could schedule an informational interview to help you learn more about the internship application process. Be sure to mention the interview will take 45–60 minutes. Preferably this should be a face-to-face interview, but if distances preclude that opportunity you could do it over the phone. Feel free to use the questions included on the Informational Interview Form (Application 3.4).

Application 3.4: Informational Interview Form

The following is a list of questions you could ask during your informational interview. The purpose of the interview is to help you prepare for your internship; therefore only ask those questions most relevant to you. Add additional questions if they will be more applicable.

- How should a prospective intern make contact with you and your agency?

_____

_____

- What criteria do you use to choose prospective interns to interview?

_____

_____

- How do you notify prospective interns about their interview time?

_____

_____

- What could a prospective intern do to prepare for their interview with you?

_____

_____

- What should a prospective intern bring with them to the interview?

_____

_____

- Is it important for interviewees to obtain information about your agency in advance?

_____

_____

- What do you look for in a cover letter?

_____

_____

- What do you look for in a résumé?

_____

_____

- What kind of interviews do you normally utilize (e.g., one-on-one, panel)?

_____

_____

- What is the proper attire for someone interviewing with your organization?

_____

_____

- What are some examples of questions you often ask interviewees?

_____

_____

- Do you prefer situational or problem-solving questions?

_____

_____

- Do applicants need any specialized credentials, such as First Aid or CPR?

_____

_____

- How long do your interviews usually last?

_____

_____

- How much importance do you place upon written reference letters?

_____

_____

- What kind and how many references do you recommend?

_____

_____

- What things can an applicant do during the application process to enhance their chances of securing an internship with your agency?

_____

_____

- Describe the process you use to make your hiring decision.

_____

_____

- Does anyone assist you in making hiring decisions on interns?

_____

_____

- Should the applicant send a thank-you letter after an interview? If so, what should it say?

_____

_____

- Can you provide any additional information that would assist me in the hiring/employment process?

_____

_____

Be creative and ask additional questions that get you the information you want.

Research

As President Obama stated, "Making your mark on the world is hard. If it were easy, everybody would do it. But it's not. It takes patience, it takes commitment, and it comes with plenty of failure along the way. The real test is not whether you avoid this failure, because you won't. It's whether you let it harden or shame you into inaction, or whether you learn from it; whether you choose to persevere." Finding the best internship is not easy, it is hard. It is a marathon, not a sprint. It takes dedication and determination—but if you persevere, you will be successful. Your journey is almost but not quite complete. You have prioritized your needs and you have established your top 10 list. Now it is time to focus very carefully on your list. Just like March Madness, the process of selecting an internship site should place considerable scrutiny on the top ten contenders. By applying your own specific criteria, you should be able to whittle the list to your "final four."

To determine the value of each potential internship, you need to find out as much as possible about each organization. What are they looking for in an intern? What experiences do they offer an intern? How much mentoring will an intern receive? When was the last time they hired one of their interns? Questions such as these and other additional information garnered about your list of potential internship sites will determine if you will actually *apply* with that agency. Remember what we have previously discussed: your game plan will provide you with a strategy for your career in sport business, but it *must* begin with a *quality* internship. Be selective. If an agency doesn't provide the experience that will help you achieve your game plan, or if the internship experience won't be a *quality* one, then eliminate it from your list.

Your research is crucial—it enables you to get the information you need to select your internship site. It also allows you to show the "best you" to potential internship supervisors. Internship supervisors are looking for well-prepared students who can sell themselves and their abilities. Gaining information about a potential internship agency before an interview will give you an edge in your quest for the best possible internship.

The Internet

As it was when you were conducting your initial search, the Internet is one of the best resources to collect information about your potential internship agencies. All sport business organizations will have a web site. If you find one that doesn't have a web site, little warning bells should begin ringing in your head along with an announcement that states "stay away… if this agency isn't current enough to have a web site, they aren't the type of location I want to investigate." Every organization involved in sport business recognizes the value of an Internet presence. They will use their web site to promote and advertise their business. In addition, they all recognize it is the most utilized source of information for potential employees and interns. In most cases, the information on an organization's web site is current and up-to-date.

University Files and Resources

Since the advent of the Internet, paper files on internship organizations that your university possesses are usually somewhat dated. Employees have come and gone, and sometimes the agency has changed dramatically since the last bit of published information. If you haven't been able to find specific information using the organization's web site, check with your internship coordinator to see if files exist for the agencies on your list. If so, make sure that the materials are thorough and up-to-date. If no files exist or the materials are out-of-date, you may have to make direct contact with the agency to gather the information you need.

Telephone Calls

Picking up the phone and actually placing a call is so "old school," but in many situations, it is an excellent method to solicit information about a sport business. Information contained on a company's web site may not be specific enough for what you are trying to find. For example, who does your cover letter and résumé need to be sent to? Speaking to an agency representative can provide you with other relevant information, such as who will actually be conducting the interviews. How many internships are still available? Have all the interns been selected? Remember the old adage "you can never undo a negative first impression." Whoever you speak to at the sport agency will form an impression about you based on how professional you are on the phone. Be polite; oftentimes the person who answers the phone is a "gatekeeper" who screens unwanted phone calls. You need this person on your side! Know exactly the type of information you are requesting. The "gatekeeper" may pass along your call to someone in more authority, so be prepared to sell yourself. In the event you are transferred directly to a potential internship supervisor, he or she may want to conduct an internship interview right on the spot. However, it is better to explain that you are still researching agencies and would prefer to set up a formal interview at a later date. Unless you are certain that this agency is ideal for you, it is important not to make commitments during your research process.

Voice Mail

You need to be prepared to leave a message via voice mail if the person you wish to speak with is unavailable. You may even want to write down and practice (do not read) your voice mail message prior to phoning a prospective internship agency. In your voice mail message, introduce yourself and give your complete phone number. Give a clear and concise message, perhaps including who referred you or how you learned about the agency. At the end of the message, you may want to repeat your name and phone number again. Be sure to thank the person, and then hang up promptly. Throughout your message, speak slowly and distinctly so the person has time to write down the information you provide. If you leave your phone number for someone to call you back, make sure *your* voice mail greeting is professional in content and tone.

Mail

Everyone today is familiar with email; unfortunately, not everyone uses it effectively. Similar to writing a letter, the email message needs to be clear, understandable, and grammatically correct with *no* spelling errors! We recommend that you type out the message using your computer's word processing software (most people use MS Word) and then cut and paste to your email message. Nothing sends a worse first impression than nonsensical sentences with multiple spelling errors. Many individuals in the sport industry will trash such a message without even bothering to send a reply. Another "no-no" is to assume the person you are emailing is a "texting fiend." Do *not* use the abbreviations we all use when texting or twittering each other. It is okay to use these short-cuts when emailing a friend, but they have *no* place in the professional world of sport business.

Obviously, when sending an email it is paramount to know an accurate email address as well as the appropriate person to send your message to. In addition, some students have the mistaken impression that everyone accesses their email 24/7; that isn't reality, so don't expect an immediate reply. On the other hand, don't wait indefinitely for a response. The best technique to use is to make a follow-up telephone call 3–4 days later. Tell the individual that you are checking to make sure the agency received your request for information. If the information has not yet been sent, ask when you might expect to receive it. There is nothing wrong with a follow-up phone call. In most situations, it demonstrates your persistence and interest. A word of caution: there is a difference between persistence and stalking. One phone call 3–4 days later is okay—3–4 phone calls every day is not!

Internship (Job) Description

Some sport business organizations utilize "job descriptions" for their internship positions. These can be extremely valuable while you search for potential internships. The information contained in these announcements can be extremely educational and can help you to decide if this opportunity meets your needs. Most sport business internship descriptions contain the following:

- Description of the position—this will provide an general overview of the position and what is expected of a potential intern.
- Responsibilities/duties:
  - Key tasks an intern will be expected to perform in relation to that specific internship.
  - Other nonessential duties an intern may be asked to perform, but which are not essential to the specific internship.
- Education—level of education (i.e., class standing) required to qualify for the internship. Also may state what type of major is required (i.e., sport management or business).

- Experience—types of experiences that the agency will expect interns to have accrued in order to succeed in the internship.
- Work schedule—the minimum number of hours required to meet expectations of the agency.
- Application process—the procedure used in applying for the internship. In most cases, sport organizations require that internships be completed for credit.
- Due date—the date all internship-related materials need to be received by the agency.
- Agency description—the agency might include some information about the agency, their philosophy, programs, services, and demographic information.

Once you receive a copy of the internship description, take the time to review it thoroughly. You might take a couple markers (e.g., yellow, blue, pink) and highlight specific responsibilities and other important information that you can use in your cover letter and, eventually, your interview. Make one of the color markers primary to highlight the most important skills and information, and another color for secondary skills and information. By doing this you will become more confident in what skills are expected of interns, as well as how you match up to those skills.

Speak with Current or Past Interns at the Agency

As Sir Francis Bacon said, "knowledge is power." The more information you can acquire about a sport business, the better you can prepare yourself. Ask your internship coordinator if anyone from your program completed their internship at the same site. If so, ask them everything you can think of that will make your decision an easier one. Items such as office politics, expectations of non-supervisors, types of ancillary responsibilities, and opportunities for part-time employment are examples of items not normally seen on job descriptions. The better you know the company, the better you will do in an interview and the better the chance that you will select the internship site that is right for you.

Volunteer at the Agency

Numerous sport management programs ask their majors to complete a specific number of "volunteer hours." Some programs term them "community service hours" and the goal of this requirement is to increase their students' realization of the importance of belonging and "giving back" to their community. Many students recognize the value these hours can be to their community and take the opportunity to give back to local sport organizations and community agencies. While involved in these experiences, some students have also come to the realization that working for a community recreation center or non-profit such as a YMCA is the type of career they wish to pursue. Volunteering at a sport organization takes a definite time commitment; however, it may prove to be mutually beneficial to you as well as to the agency. They receive much-needed assistance and you learn more about their business, including whether you would be interested in making it a career.

Student Perspective

Here are some additional comments from various sport management alumni on what they considered to be important when researching internship sites.

1. First, I spoke with my sport management professors to see if they had any connections I was not aware of that could help me secure my "dream" internship. Then I spoke with recent alums who interned with the organization I was interested in to see if they had a satisfactory experience.

2. Be creative and let your imagination run free when planning your internship and career. Consider all career paths you have an interest in and all peripheral careers that are associated with that industry. There are most likely career paths located within the industry you are looking to do an internship with that you never considered. Evaluate all perspectives of the industry before choosing a set path. Are you are interested in getting involved with the action sports industry? If so, what tours and events exist in this industry? What companies are sponsoring these events or sponsoring athletes, teams, or elements of the event? Who manages these companies—the promoters (companies putting on the event) or the actual company (e.g., Rockstar Energy Drink)? What is the

title of this position within the company (e.g., "Field Marketing Manager")? What are the steps to gain this position, and does Rockstar Energy Drink offer internships?

3. Do *not* wait till the last minute. Those who apply early for internships (December/January for a summer position) find it easier to get their foot in the door. When a company sees that an internship applicant is conscientious enough to look 5–6 months in advance for their own future, they know that will be hiring an individual who is passionate about the sport management field.

4. The number-one resource I used to find my internship opportunities was going to conferences. My senior year, I used the Stadium Managers Association seminar in Key West to secure two interviews that I had been hoping to get. I narrowed my top internships down to two different facilities, and both of the facilities sent event mangers to the conference. I tracked them down, and discussed the opportunities with them in person. It was lucky that they were both there, but even if they weren't in attendance, there were still a couple hundred other facility managers I had the opportunity to network with.

5. Another great resource was our alumni network. The list of past internships provided by our internship coordinator gave me an idea where past students did their internships. I highlighted the ones that interested me, and then I researched each one further on my own.

6. I used three different types of research techniques to start looking for an internship. Since I was doing my internship during the summer of 2007, I looked for which sports would be in season (major league and minor league baseball). I logged onto teamworkonline.com for internship postings as well as MiLB.com for a comprehensive list of clubs within the area. My first objective was to send my cover letter and résumé to every team within a seven-state area. This included all minor league as well as independent teams in Ohio, Pennsylvania, New Jersey, New York, Delaware, Virginia, and Maryland. I did this via normal mail and I received two responses for interviews. I then took the approach of emailing the marketing directors of each club in this area to see if first, any internships were available, and second, to see if I could get an interview. This led to an interview with the Delmarva Shorebirds Baseball Team, in Salisbury, MD.

Thanks to Brandon Berns, Guy Finelli, Shannon Holt, Brian Thompson, and A.J. Turkovich for the above comments.

Summary

Chapter 3 described the strategy you need to employ when deciding on an internship. The first step is to search for the appropriate site. Several key concepts must be remembered. You need to know, understand, and prioritize your professional as well as personal needs and preferences. Once you have these in mind you begin to use various resources to identify the various options. *Networking* is the most important for these resources and the power of networking can never be underestimated.

Once you have a pool of possibilities, you need to go through and see how what they have to offer meets what you hope to achieve. There are several resources at your disposal to assist in this endeavor. One reminder that we have mentioned several times in this chapter. It is imperative that you secure a *quality* internship that will allow you to employ your game plan for success. It does you no good to find an agency that uses a revolving door of unpaid interns instead of entry-level employees.

Chapter Four
Preparation: The Cover Letter

*It is common sense to take a method and try it. If it fails, admit it frankly and try another.
But above all, try something.*

---Franklin Delano Roosevelt---

In Chapter 3, we presented the idea that building your career in the world of sport business was similar to constructing a house. Let's return to that example. Chapters 1–3 dealt with the preparation for the internship, which is analogous to drawing the plans for a house, finding a location, hiring a contractor, etc. But, like our hypothetical housing project, you must have thoroughly prepared yourself for the internship experience. Go back and examine the first three chapters. Review your game plan for success. Does it still connect to your needs and preferences? Have you used all of your resources to accumulate a multitude of relevant internship locations? After prioritizing your needs and preferences, did you reduce the number of internship sites to 3–4 *quality* locations? Now that you have drawn up the proverbial blueprint, we are going to provide you with two essential tools to begin the construction of your house (career). The next two chapters discuss cover letters and résumés. These two tools are extremely important in securing an internship. However, one important caveat needs to be mentioned. The models we are providing are *examples* that over the years have proven to be successful for our students. However, it is *your* cover letter and *your* résumé. They are your tools, and it is ultimately up to you how to present yourself. If you believe you have better tools than the ones we suggest by all means feel free to use them. No matter whose examples you decide to utilize, the goal of these tools is to help you gain an internship and prepare you for a sport business career.

In many cases the cover letter is your very first contact with an internship agency. Obviously first impressions are extremely important! In 2007, a survey by Accounttemps found that "60% of executives believe a cover letter is either as important as or more critical than a résumé" (*Centre Daily Times,* August 19, 2007, p. D7). Consequently, you need to ensure that your cover letter is an excellent representation of who you are and what you can bring to the organization. If your cover letter is full of grammatical mistakes or spelling errors, the agency representative may trash it right away and never even read your résumé.

The cover letter is your opportunity to introduce yourself to a potential internship supervisor. You need to grab their attention, show that you have an in-depth knowledge about their organization, tell them exactly in what area of their business you wish to intern, impress them with your professionalism, and then let them know when you plan to contact them again. The letter must demonstrate your ability to communicate effectively in written form. Moreover, the cover letter allows you to create interest by matching your skills with the requirements of a given internship.

Format of a Cover Letter

Your cover letter must pass the "smell test"—if it smells, it will be trashed. So you need to take the time and effort to produce a letter that sounds and looks professional. Again, first impressions are extremely important. You want to engage the reader's attention and motivate them to read further. We will present several techniques throughout this chapter that will increase the quality of your cover letter. However, before the addressee even begins to read your letter, he or she has already started to form an impression. Is the address on the envelope correct? Was the letter sent to the appropriate person? Did you use their proper title? For example, say the person's name is Sandy Jones and you address it to Ms. Jones. If Sandy happens to be male, your letter might not even be read! This is an example of why thorough research is so imperative in the internship process (see chapter 3).

A cover letter should be comprised of 3–4 paragraphs and should be limited to one page. Do not make the fatal mistake of using the "shotgun approach," in which multiple letters are sent out with only the contact information being changed. Each internship location is different; therefore, be smart enough to take the time to make each cover letter specific to the location. Your internship is the first step in your game plan. In order to secure a career in the sport industry, you need to invest the time to ensure your success. Cover letters should be typed on a computer using black ink on white or gray paper. Most sport business managers aren't concerned with the weight of the paper or the cotton content. Just be sure to use quality résumé paper that can be purchased at any office supply store. Your cover letter should be printed on a laser printer.

The reader needs to be encouraged to read your entire letter, and utilizing a conventional formal letter writing layout will result in a cover letter that has "eye appeal." Also, it is important to remember that, due to the competitiveness of the sport industry as well as the perceived "value" of the particular internship experience, the agency may receive hundreds of cover letters from other internship applicants.

We have provided twelve tips that should be employed in any cover letter.

1. Each letter needs to be specific for the position you are applying for. Never use a form letter.
2. Always make the letter personal and ensure it is addressed to the person making the internship decision. This will take some research on your part.
3. Provide the contact person's full name, title, agency, and address.
4. Place an extra line between the date and address as well as between the address and the salutation. Use a colon after the salutation.
5. The letter should be no longer than one page.
6. 1" margins and single spacing should be used throughout the letter.
7. Do not repeat information contained in your résumé.
8. Be creative, but brief. Humor should be used sparingly; the reader may not think it is funny!
9. The letter should contain 3–4 paragraphs and sentences should utilize "action" verbs.
10. Three extra lines are left blank between "Sincerely," and the writer's typed name. The writer's signature goes in this space.
11. Use of "Enclosure" lets the reader know that something else is enclosed—in this case, your résumé.
12. Have someone you trust read the letter for quality control as well as to ensure they understand the information you are trying to convey.

We have provided three different examples for you of the same cover letter. While the majority of each letter is the same, each one has a slightly different look to it. Pick out the one that seems to work best for you. We have provided comments so the differences are evident. Thanks to Ben Mitchell for volunteering his letter!

SAMPLE LETTER - FORMAT #1   BLOCK

November 20, 2009 | Date is placed at left margin. |

Brenda Fitzpatrick
Associate Athletic Director
Thiel College
1 College Avenue
Greenville, PA 16125

Dear Ms. Fitzpatrick: | First word of each paragraph is NOT indented. |

I want to help bring Division I-caliber sports information to Thiel College. After a review of your school's website and publications, I strongly believe that during my internship we can establish a premiere athletic media relations office by setting and surpassing a series of comprehensive goals pertaining to the aesthetic and informational quality of athletics publications, the successful nomination of student-athletes for athletic and academic awards, and the expansion of services and features available to fans and the media via the Internet.

An internship with your athletic department will strengthen my creative and organizational skills while my strong work ethic will assist in establishing a new standard of excellence in your sports information office. While volunteering as the assistant sports information director at Saint Francis University, I was a part of tremendous advancements in all aspects of our office's performance. I will draw from that experience to foster a similar increase at Thiel. The opportunity of an internship at Thiel College will allow me to learn about advancing the already solid reputation of this institution's athletic programs and raising the expectations regarding athletic communications among the Thiel community.

I believe that the combination of my practical experience and commitment to success sets me apart from other internship applicants. Thank you for your consideration. I will be in contact with you a week from now to discuss an internship opportunity at Thiel College.

Thank you for your time and consideration.

Sincerely,

Benjamin I. Mitchell | Address is placed directly below the name. |
145 East Church Street | Phone number and email address are included. |
Homer City, PA 15748
724.434.9834
Ben.mitchell@aol.com

Enclosure: Résumé

SAMPLE LETTER - FORMAT #2   BLOCK (ALTERNATE)

> Address and contact information are at the top and indented about two-thirds across the page for balance.

145 East Church Street
Homer City, PA 15748
724.434.9834
Ben.mitchell@aol.com

November 20, 2009

Brenda Fitzpatrick
Associate Athletic Director
Thiel College
1 College Avenue
Greenville, PA 16125

Dear Ms. Fitzpatrick: Rest of letter is same as SAMPLE LETTER #1.

I want to help bring Division I-caliber sports information to Thiel College. After a review of your school's website and publications, I strongly believe that during my internship we can establish a premiere athletic media relations office by setting and surpassing a series of comprehensive goals pertaining to the aesthetic and informational quality of athletics publications, the successful nomination of student-athletes for athletic and academic awards, and the expansion of services and features available to fans and the media via the Internet.

An internship with your athletic department will strengthen my creative and organizational skills while my strong work ethic will assist in establishing a new standard of excellence in your sports information office. While volunteering as the assistant sports information director at Saint Francis University, I was a part of tremendous advancements in all aspects of our office's performance. I will draw from that experience to foster a similar increase at Thiel. The opportunity of an internship at Thiel College will allow me to learn about advancing the already solid reputation of this institution's athletic programs and raising the expectations regarding athletic communications among the Thiel community.

I believe that the combination of my practical experience and commitment to success sets me apart from other internship applicants. Thank you for your consideration. I will be in contact with you a week from now to discuss an internship opportunity at Thiel College.

Thank you for your time and consideration.

Sincerely,

Benjamin I. Mitchell

Enclosure: Résumé

SAMPLE LETTER - FORMAT #3   MODIFIED BLOCK

> Date indented about two-thirds across the page.   November 20, 2009

Brenda Fitzpatrick
Associate Athletic Director
Thiel College
1 College Avenue
Greenville, PA 16125

Dear Ms. Fitzpatrick: > First word of each paragraph indented five spaces.

    I want to help bring Division I-caliber sports information to Thiel College. After a review of your school's website and publications, I strongly believe that during my internship we can establish a premiere athletic media relations office by setting and surpassing a series of comprehensive goals pertaining to the aesthetic and informational quality of athletics publications, the successful nomination of student-athletes for athletic and academic awards, and the expansion of services and features available to fans and the media via the Internet.

    An internship with your athletic department will strengthen my creative and organizational skills while my strong work ethic will assist in establishing a new standard of excellence in your sports information office. While volunteering as the assistant sports information director at Saint Francis University, I was a part of tremendous advancements in all aspects of our office's performance. I will draw from that experience to foster a similar rise at Thiel. The opportunity of an internship at Thiel College will allow me to learn about advancing the already solid reputation of this institution's athletic programs and raising the expectations regarding athletic communications among the Thiel community.

    I believe that the combination of my practical experience and commitment to success sets me apart from other internship applicants. Thank you for your consideration. I will be in contact with you in one week to discuss an internship opportunity at Thiel College.

    Thank you for your time and consideration.

                Sincerely,

> Entire signature block indented the same number of spaces as the date.   Benjamin I. Mitchell
130 East Church Street
Homer City, PA 15748
725.434.9934
Ben.mitchell@yahoo.com

Enclosure: Résumé

Contents of a Cover Letter

The body of a cover letter has three important parts, and they are each represented by separate paragraphs. The three parts of a well-prepared cover letter are the introduction, the connection, and the closing.

Introduction

The first paragraph needs to grab the attention of the reader. Many sport organizations receive dozens of cover letters each week. You need to make yours different so they are encouraged to learn more about you. The opening lines of some student's cover letters are, for lack of a better term, "lame." They show no independent thought, no creativity, and in some cases cause the reader to want to quit before they go any further. This paragraph's primary function is to create a favorable impression and to emphasize your interest in an internship with his or her agency. Let's play role reversal for a moment. You are now the internship supervisor for a sport organization and you open a letter that states the following:

I am a senior who will be completing my degree in sport management at Alpine University. In order to complete my degree, I am required to do a minimum 480-hour internship. I am writing to inquire about the opportunities available for an internship with your organization.

What would you think? To begin with, the phrase *"I am required"* doesn't sound as if the writer is very enthusiastic about completing an internship. It sounds as if they are being forced. Let's move on the last few words, *"with your organization."* That sounds as if the student may be using a form letter. They haven't even been attentive enough to name the specific agency they are applying to! This is an example of a very boring opening paragraph. Let's look at a second example.

Please consider this letter and résumé as an indication of my interest in a summer internship with the UNP Athletic Department. I am currently a senior sport management major at Alpine University and will be graduating in August with a B.S. degree in Sport Management.

We used this type of an opening sentence in our résumés 30 years ago—do you think a sport agency might have seen one or two like this since then? What about the phrase, *"as an indication of my interest"*? They might just as well have said, "I can't come up with anything creative, but don't let that impact your decision about me"! Now let's look at a couple of creative examples.

"The thrill of life is just beginning. When you get that urge, hop on that plane and go. Chase your dreams and don't look back." I believe that this quote accurately describes my passion for life and sport, which would make me an excellent candidate for an internship position with the Adams City Sports Council.

Using a quotation is an excellent strategy to grab the attention of a reader. In this situation it was a quotation used by the writer's favorite high school teacher. In case you haven't noticed, we have used numerous quotations throughout this manual. Quotations evoke emotion and many times provide a common ground for the reader and writer to talk about. Here is a final example.

During my volunteer experience with the Altoona Curve in May 2008, I worked with Mr. James Carpenter. He told me how much he learned working for you and that in his opinion you are one of the best media relations directors in minor league baseball. Enjoying your mentorship during my internship would prove invaluable to my career.

This strategy is an example of what we call a "name dropper." The student used the name of an individual the internship supervisor knew and respected. Regardless of whether you use a strategy like the "quotation" or "name dropper" approach, you need to get the attention of the reader and make them want to read further.

Connection

The second paragraph should establish a connection between the needs of the organization and your accomplishments. You need to be able to reveal your knowledge of the agency to the potential internship supervisor and how your skills and career interests match the agency's needs. You need to stimulate their interest without repeating a lot of the information contained in your résumé. The connection paragraph must stimulate the interest of the reader. Thoroughly researching the agency beforehand will allow you to determine this information (see chapter 3).

You also need to be able to explain to the reader why this particular internship will be valuable to you.

Specific knowledge you wish to gain from the sport organization should be discussed and you must emphasize how the acquired skills will be important to you. If there are multiple internship opportunities available with the sport organization, take this time to describe exactly which one you are interested in. You do not want to appear desperate and willing to take any offer.

Closing

The last paragraph is a "call for action." You want them to know what you plan to do next. You must notify the potential internship supervisor how you plan to follow up. Do not make the rookie mistake of telling them to call you. All of the individuals at the sport business you are writing to have jobs and none of them entails calling you back. You take the initiative to tell them when you plan to call back. Also, this is where you need to specifically ask for an interview. Whatever happens, do not demand an interview. However, be careful what you ask for. If you live in Ohio and the agency is in Texas, they may ask you to come for an interview. In this situation you need to request a telephone interview. On the other hand, realize that traveling from Ohio to Texas for an interview would in most cases demonstrate your serious interest and commitment to the sport organization. Let's look at a poor example and an excellent example of what we have been talking about.

My résumé and references are enclosed for your consideration. I can be reached at 724.748.1111 or by email at idontcare@donthireme.com.

That type of a closing sentence is a prime example of how *not* to close a cover letter. A better example would be:

I will be in Orlando during Spring Break, from Friday 3/9 to Sunday 3/19, and would I like to set up an interview with you while I am there. I will contact you by Tuesday 2/28 to discuss this possibility.

As you undoubtedly can ascertain the second example is a much better way to end your letter. Finally, as in previous chapters, we want you to read some comments from a previous sport management student. This particular alumnus has been working as an event manager for a large NHL arena since 2002.

1. *In the cover letter, if you really want the job, do not tell ME to contact YOU. I'm not the one asking for a job or internship, so why would I find time to call you?*

2. *You can always contact me to find out what other materials might be needed or what the next steps in the process are.*

3. *Are you motivated and determined enough to stay focused on what you need to do to get the job? Anyone who says they "don't want to ever sell" in the sport industry is dead wrong... selling the idea of YOU is vital!*

4. *Pick up the phone and make sure that I received your materials. While you have me on the phone, be sure to ask some questions. No questions tell me you are either not interested or not prepared.*

5. *Do not presume that I check email at all hours; just call me and at least leave a voice mail. If I don't answer it, call again in a few days. Don't wait for a few weeks or month for me to get back to you.*

Final Tips and Reminders about the Cover Letter

1. Conduct the appropriate research to determine the specific person your letter needs to be sent to. Double and triple check the spelling of their name and appropriate gender.

2. Follow-up by phone within one week of the letter's arrival to discuss the possibility of an interview.

3. Your envelope is the first item that represents you. Make certain the outside is accurate and free of spelling errors. First impressions can assist or hinder the entire internship process.

4. It is not only *what* you say, but *how* you say it that is important. Attention to detail is paramount for most sport business managers. Your ability to communicate through the written word goes a long way to define your value to the organization. Make your cover letter count!

Application

Application 4.1 will help you to determine your expertise in understanding both format and content of a cover letter.

Application 4.1: Find Errors and Omissions

Sally Terrible
102 Hill Dr
Hilly, CO 80401
sst3333@essc.edu

October 25, 2011

Ms. Stephanie Salamis
Eagle Landing
1880 Eagle Landing Parkway
Grove City, FL 32003

Dear Mr. Salamis,

I am getting ready to graduate from Eastern Slope State College, with my bachelor's degree in Sport Management. I need to find an internship in order to graduate. After looking around, I feel an internship with your organization would be a good move.

I have recently completed a practicum experience with Indiana University of Pennsylvania's Student Recreation Center. During the practicum I assisted the Facility Director in implimenting new procedures for employees to clean up the facility and make sure all the equipment is clean and working properly. During my practicum, I realized very few employees at the Recreation Center follow any type of procedure to inspect the facility, which causes the members of the center to be under the risk of an injury or may-be disaster. Along with the four practicum, I also participed on the Eastern Slope State College Women's Softball team. Being an active member on the team provided me with skills such as determination, leadership, teamwork, time management, and the ability to hadle stressful situations. With all of these skills I believe I can be a benefit to the Eagle Landing Internship program.

My attached resume contains information outlining additional experiences I have within the field. Thank you for your time and consideration for the intern position with Eagle Landing. My phone number is 304.108.1363. Call me anytime. I look forward to speaking with you.

Sincerely,

Sally Terrible

Answers to Application 4.1

Sally Terrible
102 Hill Dr
Hilly, CO 80401
sst3333@unc.edu

> Address and contact information should be indented about two-thirds across the page for balance. Name should not be included.

October 25, 2011

Ms. Stephanie Salamis
Eagle Landing
1880 Eagle Landing Parkway
Grove City, FL 32003

Dear Mr. Salamis,

> Is it Ms. or Mr.?

> Use colon, not comma.

> Unenthusiastic opening paragraph; she makes it sound as if the internship is a chore. Why would ANYONE want to hire this person as an intern?

I am getting ready to graduate from Eastern Slope State College, with my bachelor's degree in Sport Management. I need to find an internship in order to graduate. After looking around, I feel an internship with your organization would be a good move.

I have recently completed a practicum experience with Indiana University of Pennsylvania's Student Recreation Center. During the practicum I assisted the Facility Director in implimenting new procedures for employees to clean up the facility and make sure all the equipment is clean and working properly. During my practicum, I realized very few employees at the Recreation Center follow any type of procedure to inspect the facility, which causes the members of the center to be under the risk of an injury or may-be disaster. Along with the four practicum, I also participated on the Eastern Slope State College Women's Softball team. Being an active member on the team provided me with skills such as determination, leadership, teamwork, time management, and the ability to hadle stressful situations. With all of these skills I believe I can be a benefit to the Eagle Landing Internship program.

> Sentence structure in second paragraph is sloppy, rambling, vague, and uninformative.

> Should not hyphenate "may-be."

My attached resume contains information outlining additional experiences I have within the field. Thank you for your time and consideration for the intern position with Eagle Landing. My phone number is 303.297.1363. Call me anytime. I look forward to speaking with you.

Sincerely,

> No "call for action"… asked Stephanie to call her!

> THREE spelling errors! "implimenting," "participed," and "hadle"

Sally Terrible

> What "four practicum"? Never mentioned anything about them.

> Did not indicate a résumé was enclosed.

Examples of Spell-Check Malfunctions

You all realize the importance of using spell-check to alleviate obvious spelling errors. However, what happens when someone uses spell-check but doesn't take the time to proofread the material? Well, we thought that you might like to see several of the "oops" mistakes some of our students have made. Unfortunately, each of these went out in actual cover letters, most of which resulted in a failed internship search.

1. I worked within budgetary restraints on a daily bases.
2. My concession strand employees were highly motivated by me.
3. I planed and coordinated multiple youth events.
4. I was able to attend a number of premises liability trails.
5. I was the assistant manger for a local minor league baseball team.
6. While working in the box office I dealt with problems and questions the quests had
7. I made sure no one entered the players licker room who was not authorized

Sample Cover Letters

We have provided five cover letters for you to review. However, it is important to remember that a cover letter is a personal tool. You need to utilize a format that you believe represents you the best. Use ours for guidance, but be sure to write *your* letter in your own style and wording. Several of these letters were written by prospective interns in the past 3–5 years. Some may deviate slightly from the guidelines we previously presented. But, as we said, your cover letter is a personal tool; it is not essential that your letters conform *exactly* to our guidelines. One vital piece of advice, however: it is important that all necessary information is included in a neat, well-formatted, and error-free cover letter.

SAMPLE COVER LETTER #1

January 5, 2011

Alison Barber
Disney's Wide World of Sports
120 Main St.
Tallahassee, FL 34758

Dear Ms. Barber:

Famous baseball pitcher Tommy John once exclaimed, "Always give one hundred percent and you will never second guess yourself." This quote is an excellent description of my dedication to completing tasks. I am in my final semester at Penn State University, preparing for a sport management internship. After extensive research, I believe the summer event management internship you offer at Disney's Wide World of Sports would allow me to gain invaluable experience with an excellent organization.

Working for Disney's Wide World of Sports would allow me to realize my dream of becoming an effective event coordinator. I have worked for LiveNation at the Pittsburgh Post-Gazette Pavilion for the past three summers, where I have had the opportunity to witness firsthand the tremendous amount of work that an event entails. The lessons learned at PGP will allow me to interact effectively with event coordinators with Disney. I have received positive feedback from professors, peers, and employers regarding my dedication to event management and my never-ending search for advancement. My senior-level classes have allowed me to experience leadership positions and personalized leadership and management training. My dedication to my future career in event management, positive attitude, and passion for success would make me an excellent candidate for your internship with Disney's Wide World of Sports.

I believe the combination of my practical experience and commitment to success sets me apart from other candidates. I will be in Orlando during Spring Break, from Monday 3/9 to Saturday 3/14 and I would like to set up an interview with you while I am there. I will contact you by Tuesday 2/28 to discuss this possibility. Thank you for your consideration.

Sincerely,

Brian A. Thompson
1080 Oakdale Drive
Pottsville, PA 19075
412-409-3702
rmj4465@sru.edu

Enclosure: Résumé

SAMPLE COVER LETTER #2

44 Rocky Top Road
Cold Springs, PA 18432
843-230-3872
tsj1208@sru.edu

September 26, 2011

Ms. Adeline Watts
Guest Services/Tour Manager
PSSI Stadium Corporation
30 Rooney Ave.
Pittsburgh, PA 15210

Dear Ms. Watts:

I have recently completed a 100-hour practical experience with the Pittsburgh Steelers' Ticket Office with Ben Lentz. Mr. Lentz notified me of the PSSI internships in event operations for the 2010 spring semester. I am very interested in applying for the internship you have available. I believe this internship would be a very valuable experience to me, and I feel that my background makes me a valuable candidate for this position.

I have over 170 hours of volunteer and practical experience with Keystone High School's Athletic Department as an event supervisor and assistant to the Athletic Director. I was responsible for supervising and assisting 15 volunteers who helped set up and operate ticket, merchandise, and concession sales during varsity and junior high football contests. I have also completed a facility and event management class at Slippery Rock University, where I helped organize and manage an effective charity golf outing benefiting Hurricane Katrina victims. Finally, I am familiar with the Pittsburgh Steelers organization because of my experience in the ticket office. I believe my understanding of the stadium policies, in addition to having to field over 100 customer service questions daily, makes me an ideal candidate for this position.

I would appreciate any opportunity to discuss this internship position. I plan to contact you in a week to discuss this exciting opportunity, and I look forward to speaking with you. Thank you for your time and consideration.

Sincerely,

Anthony M. Smith

Enclosure: Résumé

SAMPLE COVER LETTER #3

August 2, 2009

Walter Thimbleton
Director of Corporate & Suite Sales
Cleveland Curve Baseball Club
300 South Main Street
Cleveland, OH 44308

Dear Mr. Thimbleton:

According to renowned entrepreneur Richard Branson, "a business has to be involving, it has to be fun, and it has to exercise your creative instincts." This quote exemplifies my attraction to minor league baseball because of the fun, interactive, everyday environment.

I possess a fervent interest in your game-day operations/community relations internship with the Cleveland Curve. I have had extensive experiences with a variety of game-day operations that are important to the success of events. These include the setup of athletic facilities and the initial planning of an event. I would undoubtedly use these skills during my internship with the Curve. In addition, I have accumulated over 200 volunteer hours in my community, which has allowed me to interact with diverse groups. These experiences have spurred my interest in continuing my community involvement. I believe my creativity will assist me in contributing to the atmosphere of the Cleveland Curve baseball club.

I have enclosed a copy of my most recent résumé for your review. I plan to contact you within the next week to confirm that you have received my résumé and to discuss the possibility of my driving to Cleveland for an interview. Thank you for your time. I am eager to demonstrate my interest for an internship with the Curve.

Sincerely,

Christina Clementi
1930 Washington Avenue
Yorkshire, PA 15885
803-882-2611
aot8300@sru.edu

Enclosure: Résumé

SAMPLE COVER LETTER #4

Rebecca Morgan

Campus Address	**Permanent Address**
526 Vineyard Circle	4242 Riverside Drive
Slippery Rock, PA 16057	Crownsville, MD 21045
440.317.4315	410.441.8809

November 12, 2011

Jon Babcock
Director of Operations
D.C. United - RFK Stadium
48 West Capitol St. SE
Washington, D.C. 20003

Dear Mr. Babcock:

Dr. Robin Ammon told me about your internship opening with D.C. United. I believe that I would be a good fit because of my prior experience, as well as my passion for soccer. I believe working in operations for D.C. United would also allow me to gain great experience in stadium management. I would also enjoy giving back to an organization that I truly believe in.

During the summer of 2009, I worked for the Baltimore Blast, a professional indoor soccer team. I gained experience in marketing, operations, and public relations, areas I would also be expected to assist with as an intern with United. My experience with the Blast will help me with the match production aspect of the D.C. United internship. In 2010, I worked with ASG sports, located in Baltimore, MD. They provide event services and manage the events from concept to completion. I was able to gain experience working directly with various clients by overseeing registration at five Chick-fil-A youth soccer clinics. I believe that these experiences have enhanced my organizational skills and made me more detail-oriented. These skills are ideal for the operations and logistics aspect of the D.C. United internship.

I believe that completing an internship with D.C. United would be a wonderful opportunity for me to grow as a sport manager. I would love to speak to you about an internship with United. I will contact you directly about the opportunity by the end of the week.

Sincerely,

Becky Morgan

Enclosure: Résumé

SAMPLE COVER LETTER #5

MARY FITZPATRICK
Fitzy33@yahoo.com

Local Address	*Permanent Address*
100 Bakerstown Rd	*18 Eaglecrest Dr.*
Golden, CO 80401	*Lakewood, CO 80226*
303-237-6534	*303-928-4707*

October 16, 2011

Ms. Nikkie Reid
Manager
Better Bodies Fitness Center
7777 West Jewell Ave.
Lakewood, CO 80232

Dear Ms. Reid:

I have been involved for many years with cross country and lacrosse, and now I am eager to start my career in the fitness industry. Dr. Joel Sakowski, at UC-Denver, notified me that you are a graduate of our sport management program. Please consider me a candidate for an internship with your Better Bodies location during this coming fall semester. Our 12-credit, 480-contact-hour internships may begin anytime after September 7th and must be completed by December 10th.

I have been a member at the Westminster Better Bodies location since 2005, and I have a good understanding of that facility and its management. My previous athletic experience has provided the opportunity to visit and utilize a variety of facilities across the United States, and I have worked with a diverse range of individuals. During my internship, I hope to learn more about the management of your center, including the budgeting process, membership sales, marketing, and advertising. I have absolutely no doubt that an internship with Better Bodies will allow me to gain a better understanding of the overall fitness industry, as well as provide me with the opportunity to network with a variety of fitness managers.

Your mentorship during my internship experience will be invaluable and I would relish the chance to speak with you further. I will be contacting you next week to discuss a convenient time for you to meet with me. Thank you.

Sincerely,

Mary Fitzpatrick

Enclosure: Résumé

Summary

A cover letter is a personal tool, and therefore you must be comfortable with both its content and format. This chapter has provided information, applications, and examples for writing your cover letter. The importance of a well-prepared cover letter can't be overstated. It is most often the first contact a sport business has with you. That first impression must be a memorable one.

The cover letter is one of two important tools used in securing an internship; the cover letter introduces the résumé to a prospective internship supervisor. The cover letter and résumé work hand in hand and, if properly written, will increase your chances of securing the internship you desire.

Chapter 5 provides you with the requisite information necessary to create a first-class résumé. Similar to chapter 4, the next chapter will provide both applications and examples so you may witness the components required for a professional résumé. When coupled with a well-written cover letter, a high-quality résumé creates a powerful tool that will aid you in your journey towards a career in sport business!

Chapter Five
Preparation: The Résumé

What lies behind us and what lies before us are tiny matters compared to what lies within us.

---Ralph Waldo Emerson---

A quality résumé will take a great deal of thought, multiple drafts, and a lot of work. But it is one of the two most important tools to build your house (career). Unfortunately, right or wrong, good or bad, some individuals in sport business will only give your cover letter a cursory glance and go immediately to your résumé. Therefore, of the two tools, the résumé is *the* most critical. This chapter will describe how to create a quality résumé that, in conjunction with your previously written cover letter (see chapter 4), will give you a devastating one-two punch! As in previous chapters, we will provide examples of well-written résumés and include some student suggestions as well.

The word 'résumé' comes from the French word for 'summary.' And that is exactly what it is—a summary of all of your experiences, skills, achievements, and interests. However, do *not* make the mistake of believing that it is all a résumé is. It is imperative to remember that your résumé is a tool—a *marketing* tool. Along with the interview (covered in chapter 6), your résumé provides you with an opportunity to sell yourself to a potential sport organization. A well-organized, attractive, and informative résumé will help you to secure the best possible internship.

One concept that must be kept in mind is that a well-written cover letter and high-quality résumé will *not* secure a job. If properly written, the two tools *might* get you an interview. Put yourself in the position of a sport business executive. Would you hire someone based on what you read on several sheets of paper? If you did so, you wouldn't have a job for very long, because some individuals misrepresent themselves. Therefore, the goal of your cover letter and résumé should be to gain an interview.

Similar to your cover letter, your résumé must be well-written, with proper sentence structure, appropriate grammar and punctuation and absolutely *no* spelling errors! Will a well-written résumé guarantee you an internship? Maybe not, but a poorly written one will certainly eliminate you from consideration! A properly prepared résumé will attract the reader's attention and go a long way toward securing the interview you need.

As we mentioned at the beginning of chapter 4, we provide you with numerous examples and strategies that have assisted our previous students. Conversely, you need to remember that the individual reading your résumé has his or her own personal preferences regarding the format and content of a résumé. For example, in recent years it has become apparent that some sport industry representatives expect a one-page résumé. We don't concur with this line of thinking. We have had hundreds of interns and have spoken extensively to multiple internship supervisors and believe a two-page résumé is the best method. We believe it would be impossible to provide evidence of appropriate preparation, multiple previous experiences, and powerful references all on one page. We will provide a couple of one-page examples, but our recommendation would be to stay with a two-page résumé. On the other hand, for an entry-level position it is inappropriate to have more than two pages.

We need to briefly mention another misconception. Some students believe that they complete an internship and then immediately move on to a career. Not so fast, my fine young friends. You may need to complete additional internships, depending on the area of the sport industry that interests you. Some sport organizations look for higher levels of experience than can be garnered during a single internship. In 2006, an informal survey of college students by Vault Inc. found that 53% had completed two or more internships by the summer after graduation. Thirty-one percent completed one and 16% did not complete an internship (USA Today, May 15, 2006, B-1). Therefore having a quality résumé will be even more valuable for a student required to complete multiple internships.

The "Master Résumé"

Chapter 4 mentioned the importance of writing different cover letters for each specific internship position—the reason being that no two internships are the same. Therefore, each cover letter must be specific to the position you are applying for. The same can be said for your résumé. Regrettably, most students have one résumé, and they send it out for every internship or job they apply for. This is analogous to using a baseball to play football, basketball, and lacrosse. Each of those sports uses a ball, but each ball is designed specifically for the sport. Would you be as skilled in basketball if you had learned the game with a baseball? We would imagine your dribbling skills *might* be a little counterproductive! The same can be said for your résumé. If you utilize the same résumé when applying to a sport marketing company as you do when applying for a facility operation position, your skill set will prove counterproductive. A sport marketing company is not looking for the same expertise as a sport facility.

We suggest you create two documents when creating your résumé. One is an accumulation of *all* your relevant sport management experiences, education, other work experiences, achievements, certificates, workshops and seminars attended as well as potential references. This will become your "master résumé." Do not worry about the format. Just put information down. Some of this information may seem irrelevant; however, experience teaches us there may be times when you will use this information. It is always better to be prepared. You will draw from this information to create the second document, your "professional résumé."

Application

Application 5.1 is called the Master Résumé Worksheet. Use this worksheet to list all information about yourself that might be useful to a prospective internship supervisor. Later, you can use this "master résumé" to pick and choose any combination of information or facts that meet the criteria for the specific internship (or employment) position you are seeking. After you select the information you need, you can begin to polish the content in preparation for your "professional résumé."

Application 5.1: Master Résumé Worksheet

Name, Address, Phone numbers, Email (local and permanent)

_____

_____

_____

_____

_____

_____

Career Objective (use your game plan for success)

_____

_____

_____

_____

_____

_____

Relevant Sport Management Experiences (paid or unpaid)

_____

_____

_____

_____

_____

_____

Education (list post-secondary experiences)

_____

_____

_____

_____

_____

Workshops/Seminars Attended

_____

_____

_____

_____

_____

Work (non-sport) Experience

_____

_____

_____

_____

_____

Civil Service (non-sport volunteer experiences)

_____

_____

_____

_____

_____

Awards, Honors, Certificates

_____

_____

_____

_____

_____

Professional Memberships

_____

_____

_____

_____

References (include title or position, addresses, phone numbers, emails)

_____

_____

_____

_____

Other Pertinent Information

_____

_____

_____

_____

The "Professional Résumé"

The second document is called your "professional résumé" and traditionally is what someone thinks of when he or she hears the word "résumé." It is the two-page *specific* résumé that you will send out for each internship or career position.

Your "professional résumé" may reflect one of several types of styles. A *chronological résumé* lists specific experiences as they occurred. The experiences are listed from the most recent to the oldest (by date). As a sport management student, you will predominantly use this style of résumé. All of our résumé examples in this chapter will use the chronological style. However, if an individual has been out of sport for a while or if they possess gaps in their résumé, as a result of going to graduate school or being in the military, a *functional résumé* is normally used. This style of résumé documents a person's skills, knowledge, abilities, and accomplishments without emphasizing dates. If you believe a functional résumé is best for you, consult the references listed in Appendix D. Some sport organizations are beginning to require *electronic* and *scannable* résumés for full-time positions. So far, they have rarely been used for internships. These styles are normally used when a large number of applicants are expected to apply. The organization can use the "find" feature in a word processor and look for specific "buzzwords" when they are trying to compare hundreds of résumés. Information on the format and content of electronic and scannable résumés is included at the end of this chapter.

Additional Student Input

At this point you are probably ready to read some additional comments from previous sport management interns. Each student is now working in the sport industry and are relating back to their overall internship experience. There will be more such comments on both chapters 6 and 7.

1. I did *not* want to work for an organization that uses their intern to do all of their "dirty" work (making copies, stuffing envelopes, etc.). I wanted a position where there was a track record of giving their interns *real* projects where I could attain managerial experience.
2. Never let yourself think, "I won't get the internship." If you're prepared—and you want it bad enough—you'll get it.
3. Always make sure you have a backup plan that excites you as much as your top choice.
4. Get as much experience during your undergraduate degree as possible. This means trying to gain practical experience in different areas so you can determine your true passion.
5. When you know your true passion, the internship hunt is usually a little more focused and less stressful.
6. Be ready to work hard, for little/no pay and for long hours.
7. Depending on the workload requirements of your internship, budget your time well, so you can excel in your internship and turn in your work on time.
8. Do the small things really well—people notice!
9. Don't be afraid to go anywhere in the country/world for the right internship.
10. The main thought I had while looking for an internship was to find internship opportunities that were going to provide me with professional experience. I did not care where the internship was located. I just wanted a position that was going to give me the most amount of on-the-job training, so I could maximize my marketability.

Thanks to Jason Hannold, A. J. Turkovich, Dana Maalouf, and Megan Powell!

Format and Content of the Print Résumé

In order to attain the goals you established in your game plan, your résumé must be of the highest possible quality. Here are specific strategies that are paramount for your résumé:

1. *Professional Appearance.* As with your cover letter, you should use a computer to write your résumé and a laser printer to print it. Unless it is absolutely necessary, print each copy of your résumé rather than mass producing (copying) them. Unless you utilize a high-end copier, the quality of print when you make copies is not the same as when you print them individually. As with your cover letter, the paper used for your résumé should be white or gray. The quality (bond and cotton content) of paper is not of major importance. You can purchase résumé quality paper from any office supply store (Staples, Office Max, etc.). Some students believe it is necessary to have their résumé prepared and printed by a résumé expert or commercial company. This couldn't be any further from the truth. Plus, this option can be quite expensive and your results aren't guaranteed to be any different than if you did it yourself. Your résumé is *your* tool. Don't put your tool in someone else's hands.

2. *Clarity.* Do not try to be overly creative. Use words and terms that are understandable. Make certain that your sentences convey your thoughts in an effective manner. Have someone else read your résumé to ensure that they understand your intent. Your résumé should pass the "grandmother test." In other words, your grandmother should be able to read and completely understand the content of your résumé. You want to impress the sport agency with your knowledge, but don't use a lot of industry-specific jargon. The reader may be someone in the human resources with little knowledge of the terminology. Make certain that every piece of information is important and stated as briefly as possible (without violating rule #3).

3. *Thoroughness.* It is imperative that you provide a detailed list of your sport-relevant experiences. Use action verbs to express your capabilities. You want the reader to be engaged and not nodding off. Your sentences must convey that you *did* something. In order to help in this task, we have included a variety of "action verbs" later in this chapter (Resource #1). Remember to use the *chronological* style when listing your experiences. However, be careful that any gaps of time don't go unexplained. If there is a two-year gap in your experience, use your cover letter to provide the explanation.

4. *Quality Control.* There is nothing more demoralizing than to realize you submitted a document containing poorly worded sentences or, even worse, spelling errors. Aristotle said, *"We are what we repeatedly do. Excellence, then, is not an act, but a habit."* Excellence must become a habit and this will require you to edit your résumé, re-edit it, and then edit it again. There is absolutely *no* excuse for poor grammar or spelling errors. Use every possible means to eliminate errors. Use the computer's spellchecking software. *Slowly* proofread your résumé. In many cases, you have read it so often that you tend to skim the wording rather than focusing on each word. Ask a friend or relative who is proficient in English grammar to proofread your résumé. The importance of proofreading cannot be overemphasized. One poll, cited by On the Mark Media, found that "84% of executives say it takes just one typographical error in a résumé for them to remove a candidate from job consideration" (*Centre Daily Times,* February 18, 2007, p. D9).

5. *Format.* Consistency and balance are extremely important when "designing" your résumé. That is correct: we said "designing your résumé." Outside of the interview, your résumé is your best marketing tool. Like a pretty picture it must be appealing to the eye. Your margins need to be consistent. The size of font you that you employ, words you bold, headings you underline and sections you indent—these formatting tools all must be used in a consistent manner. How your résumé sits on the page is also an important consideration. No matter how you format your résumé, there will be empty areas, know as "white spaces," that contain no text. These white spaces need to be balanced for aesthetic reasons.

6. *Honesty. When in doubt, tell the truth* (Mark Twain). *Never* lie on a résumé, overstate your accomplishments, or mislead a potential internship supervisor regarding your experiences or responsibilities. A lie on your résumé will follow you throughout life. There have been countless examples where an individual made an inaccurate claim early in their career and it came back to haunt them later in life; oftentimes resulting in a loss of job. One example occurred in 2001 when, after only five days on the job, George O'Leary resigned as the head football coach at the University of Notre Dame. His departure was a direct result of an investigation by a New Hampshire newspaper and ESPN.com about several claims on his résumé that were discovered to be false. A second situation occurred in 2006, when the CEO of RadioShack resigned over allegations of false statements on his résumé (USA Today, February 21, 2006). Upon reviewing these two situations, it is imperative that you make absolutely certain that everything on your résumé is completely accurate. Don't sacrifice your future due to a mistake you make today.

7. *Prerequisites or requirements.* Does the internship require any certificates or specific courses in order to qualify for the position? If so, make certain that you include these qualifications in your cover letter and résumé. If you do not possess the necessary prerequisites or requirements, you need to find out how to obtain these documents or courses. Try to meet all requirements before applying, even though some agencies will allow an intern to start the internship while he or she is taking a prerequisite course or certificate program.

In addition to the essential information, there are many things to keep in mind when preparing a print résumé. Some of the more important ones include:

1. Readers pay the *most* attention to the beginning of a page, paragraph, sentence, or list. Therefore, be sure to structure your résumé to:
    a. Get the most important sections (e.g., profile statements, professional experiences) toward the beginning of the résumé.
    b. List experiences beginning with the most recent, working back to those in the past.
    c. Give the most relevant responsibilities or skills first.

2. Do not put personal information such as sex, height, weight, age, or marital status in your résumé.

3. Provide brief descriptions of your professional (and other) work experiences that show skills. Consider using profile statements to summarize your professional attributes. Use action verbs.

4. Make sure words in a series are in the same tense and form. Only use present tense if you are still involved in an activity or work experience. Avoid personal pronouns (e.g., I, me, he, she).

5. Do not use abbreviations/acronyms by themselves, unless they are *universally* known and accepted (e.g., EMT, CPR, postal abbreviations for states). Thus, NRPA should be listed: National Recreation and Park Association (NRPA). In general, contractions should be avoided as well.

6. Highlight headings and important information by using boldface type, italics, or underlining. These techniques add emphasis and are important to maintaining good balance on the page.

7. *Never* print (or copy) a two-page résumé back-to-back. Staple (or paper clip) the pages together in the upper left-hand corner, and be sure to include your name on page two. Also, make sure the text extends *at least* halfway down page two. If not, expand the text or reduce the résumé to one page.

8. Do not put a page break in the middle of an entry. Also, try to avoid splitting a section (e.g., professional experience) between pages. If you do split a section, be sure to put the heading with "Continued" specified on page two. "Cont'd" is also acceptable, even though it is a contraction.

9. If possible, references should be included on the résumé, and they should be the last item. If they are listed on a separate sheet of paper, it is not necessary to refer to them on the résumé.

12 Tips for a Professionally Written Résumé

We have provided a number of suggestions on how you can increase the *power* of your résumé. We would like to thank Dr. Bill Sutton from the University of Central Florida for his valuable assistance in the preparation of this list.

1. Work experience and responsibility dictate the length. Someone just starting out should have 1–1.5 pages *plus* references. *Always* include your references!

2. Use humor judiciously, as mentioned previously; you just may not be as funny as you think you are!

3. Some students waste their time with an "objective." Why? Isn't everyone's objective to gain an interview? If so, then why waste valuable space in stating the obvious?

4. Unless you were on *Good Morning America* or *20/20*, high school achievements are in most cases irrelevant.

5. Select your references with care, but always provide three or four. Be consistent with their information that you provide on the résumé. Include the person's full name, title (if appropriate), complete mailing address, phone number, and e-mail address. Do not use the same references for every position you apply for. Have a variety so you can tailor your references for specific positions. The general rule is to have one reference who can speak about your academic prowess, one who can speak about your work experiences and then what we term a *wild* card. This is an individual is carries a "wow" factor; for example a well-known athlete, a politician, or a famous member of your community. If you don't know someone like this, then double up on one of the other two types. You need a reference to provide a dynamite explanation about your abilities. They must be able to "sell" the sport organization on your potential; therefore it is critical that you always ask for their permission before listing them as a reference. Keep them updated about the various positions you are applying for. This will prevent them from being caught off-guard. Finally, make *certain* that you send them a short thank-you note for their assistance.

6. Always ask someone you trust to provide quality control and read your résumé to ensure it is understandable and conveys what you intend.

7. The quality of your résumé will impact the perception the reader forms about you. Make the first impression a good one.

8. Most résumés are looked at very briefly—some estimates say less than 30 seconds. Therefore your bullet points must be *results-based* (what you have accomplished); your résumé should *not* highlight your duties and responsibilities. Quantify your experiences (by adding numbers or percentages) and make them into *Accomplishment Statements*. A couple of examples: 1) "supervised a 400 player basketball tournament," 2) "produced 2000 media guides," 3) "provided service training to 34 staff members," 4) "updated 2400 member applications into Excel spreadsheet." These are very specific and a potential internship supervisor can easily compare your experiences to another applicant's.

9. Be cautious with providing your GPA. In many instances it is irrelevant. Grade inflation is so common that many sport agencies discount a person's GPA. However, if you have maintained a 4.0 or are consistently on the Dean's list you might wish to include it. However, do *not* put down a grade in your major—it is a complete waste of time.

10. Volunteer activities need to be identified. These are experiences, especially sport-related ones, are valuable. List them as "Civil Service."

11. You are all very skillful with computers and the various well-known software packages. However, if you are a proficient web designer or have expertise with a specialized software package relevant to the position you are applying for, be sure to highlight it on your résumé.

12. Sport has become extremely global. A foreign language competency could be the deciding factor when considered for an internship position. This type of skill is extremely valuable in today's sport industry.

Profile Statements

Some students consider using "profile statements" near the beginning of a résumé to summarize and empha-size the applicant's most positive attributes. Your résumé is your own personal tool and if you believe the use of such a statement will assist you, then by all means use one. However, we believe that if you quantify your accomplishments and pay strict attention to the proper formatting, a profile statement is irrelevant.

Commercial Résumé Preparation and Printing

In most cases, employing a professional résumé service is not only unnecessary, it can be downright expen-sive. You all have the computer savvy to successfully create a powerful résumé. You need to remember that unless you know the owner, you are just one of a hundred résumés that a company such as this produces. They are a commercial entity and are dependent on a high volume in order to show a profit. It is your résumé, why trust its design to someone else? While they would not intentionally sabotage your efforts, they don't know you and don't have the inclination to put their heart and soul into its design.

Preparing Your Print Résumé

Now we are ready to actually begin the preparation of the most important tool you have at your disposal. We provided several different resources for you to use to increase the power of your résumé. One suggestion in the previous section (Additional Tips) was to use "action verbs." Nothing becomes more laborious than read-ing a résumé that utilizes non-action verbs. Resource #1 provides a list of action verbs. Resource #2 provides several specific strategies about the format of your résumé. Since we discussed numerous tips to strengthen your résumé, the Résumé Checklist (Resource #3) will ensure that your résumé conforms to our suggestions.

You will be competing against numerous other individuals for every *quality* internship position. There-fore, your résumé needs to have the power necessary to pique the reader's interest and motivate them to read your résumé in its entirety. Since there will be numerous, sometimes hundreds, of résumés being evaluated, you need to select the style that not only meets your personality but doesn't reflect the same format as all the others. You would be surprised as to the number of students who copy someone else's résumé with no thought as to the ramifications of such an act. The planning for and creation of a *powerful* résumé takes an extensive amount of research, lots of thought, some personality, and the dedication to ensure it reflects your experiences in the best possible manner.

Resource #1—Action Verbs

Accomplished	Documented	Organized
Achieved	Edited	Participated
Adapted	Educated	Performed
Administered	Eliminated	Planned
Advanced	Employed	Prepared
Advocated	Enforced	Presented
Advised	Established	Processed
Analyzed	Evaluated	Procured
Applied	Expanded	Produced
Appointed	Expedited	Programmed
Arranged	Formed	Promoted
Assessed	Founded	Proposed
Assigned	Fulfilled	Provided
Assisted	Generated	Published
Authored	Guided	Purchased
Broadened	Handled	Recommended
Built	Hired	Redesigned
Centralized	Identified	Reduced
Charted	Implemented	Reorganized
Clarified	Improved	Represented
Coached	Increased	Researched
Collaborated	Influenced	Resolved
Collected	Initiated	Restored
Completed	Installed	Restructured
Composed	Instigated	Reviewed
Conceived	Instituted	Revised
Conceptualized	Instructed	Saved
Conducted	Integrated	Scheduled
Conserved	Interpreted	Secured
Consulted	Interviewed	Selected
Contracted	Introduced	Served
Contributed	Inventoried	Sold
Controlled	Investigated	Solved
Coordinated	Launched	Specified
Counseled	Led	Strengthened
Created	Located	Structured
Decreased	Maintained	Studied
Delivered	Managed	Suggested
Demonstrated	Marketed	Supervised
Designed	Modified	Taught
Determined	Monitored	Tested
Developed	Negotiated	Trained
Directed	Obtained	Undertook
Discovered	Operated	Utilized
Distributed	Ordered	Wrote

Resource #2—Résumé Guide

1. *Heading:* Name, current address, e-mail address, home and cell phones. If your current address is at school, you should list your permanent address as well.

2. *Education* (e.g., community college, college, university): Some individuals place this section after Relevant Work Experience. It depends on the priorities you are attempting to emphasize. *Always* include this information somewhere on the résumé. High school experiences should not be listed. *Optional:* If you come from a non-sport-management curriculum, you may find it valuable to list courses you have taken that are relevant to your internship.

3. *Computer Skills* (optional): Unless you have special knowledge or web design experience, you can normally choose to leave this section off your résumé.

4. *Relevant Sport and/or Volunteer Experience*: Depending on availability of space this category may be divided into several sections. For example you will have sport related work experience, non-sport related experience and some volunteer experience. Dividing this category may help you place the most important experiences at the beginning of a section. However, if you only have one category do not divide the category. Describe the experience according to the skills that you demonstrated in the position. In other words *quantify* the experience and make them each *accomplishment statements.* Use action verbs to create action phrases.

5. *Awards, Honors, Certificates, Licenses:* Remember not to abbreviate or use acronyms. Do not assume that the reader will be familiar with the organization. List the entire title, with the abbreviated title in parentheses.

6. *Memberships* (community/campus organizations, professional associations): Be sure to list offices held and responsibilities. These demonstrate leadership and professional development.

Note: The order of categories #3 through #6 is sometimes changed, depending upon what the applicant wants to emphasize.

Resource #3—Résumé Checklist

_____ Material fits neatly on one or two pages. If two pages, at least half of the second page is filled with text. Also, the top of page 2 includes name and the text begins with a new entry.

_____ Overall appearance is balanced (both pages), including adequate white space at top, bottom, sides, and between entries.

_____ No spelling, grammatical, or punctuation errors.

_____ Printing or typing is neat, clean, and looks professional.

_____ Name, address(es), and telephone number(s) are at the top.

_____ Writing style is concise and direct. Information is easy to read.

_____ Abbreviations or acronyms, if used, are in parentheses and proceeded by full title. Contractions and personal pronouns (e.g., I, me, my) are not used.

_____ Paragraph information is brief, to the point, and complete.

_____ Words in a series are in the same tense and form.

_____ All appropriate education, work experiences, and other information are included in the résumé.

_____ Important titles are emphasized by bold print or underlined, where appropriate, but these techniques are not overused.

_____ Indentions are appropriately used to set off information and create eye appeal and uniformity within sections.

_____ Accomplishment statements use action verbs to create action phrases.

_____ Dates are uniform, with no big gaps.

_____ Personal data (i.e., sex, height, age, marital status) are not included.

_____ Overall résumé demonstrates your ability meets the demands of the internship.

NOTE: For quality control purposes, have an additional person use this checklist on your résumé.

Sample Print Résumés

We have provided you with five different résumés to examine. Each has its own style and format. These are *real* résumés from real sport management students. Since they are for entry level positions, they each utilize the chronological format. Examine each résumé thoroughly. You may find some formats that you want to use for your own résumé. We have tried to include résumés representing a variety of specializations within the sport industry. As you read through the various examples, it is vital to remember that your résumé must be a reflection of *you. There is no absolutely perfect résumé format.*

We also included two résumés that are not good examples, and they will help you to determine your expertise in understanding both format and content of a cover letter. When looking at the different formats in our examples, notice the bold lines, lines used to separate information, and use of other techniques to emphasize specific information. These techniques add emphasis and style to the print résumé; however, be careful not to overuse such devices. If a résumé is considered too "flashy," it may result in a rejection letter.

The résumés in this manual were done inexpensively because they were prepared on a computer; however, they did take considerable time to construct. You can stay away from expensive commercial résumé preparation costs if you have access to a computer with word processing or desktop publishing software.

SAMPLE PRINT RÉSUMÉ #1

Anthony M. Smith

Address: 122 Rocky Top Road, Knox, PA 16238   **Phone:** (814) 719-8875
E-Mail: ams1989@sru.edu   **Cellular Phone:** (814) 688-3656

Education

Slippery Rock University of Pennsylvania

Bachelor of Science Degree in Sport Management

Minor in Business Administration

Expected graduation date: May 2007

Practical Experience in Sport

- **Foxburg Country Club** *(July 2006)*
  - Completed daily sales to over 40 club members and non-members
  - Calculated and balanced approximately $800 in sales on a daily basis
  - Organized and restocked over $200 worth of merchandise daily

- **Pittsburgh Steelers' Ticket Office** *(May 2006–June 2006)*
  - Processed over $100,000 worth of individual game ticket requests daily during the Pittsburgh Steelers Individual Game Sale
  - Assisted over 100 season ticket holders and general public questions per day
  - Performed data entry and data corrections to approximately 50 accounts daily in the Archtics Data System
  - Created over 2,200 return labels for Individual Game Sale applications that were unable to be filled

- **Clarion University Sports Information Department** *(May 2005–June 2005)*
  - Created and formatted 12 pages in the 2005 Clarion Football Media Guide
  - Contacted and addressed scheduling conflicts with seven Pennsylvania State Athletic Conference (PSAC) Sports Information Directors

- **Keystone High School Athletic Department** *(April 2004–May 2004)*
  - Helped create a $63,000 budget for all 19 varsity and junior high sports for the 2004–2005 school year
  - Created scheduling contracts for all 265 varsity, junior varsity and junior high sporting events for the 2004–2005 school year
  - Examined students eligibility criteria for over 80 spring sport participants and compiled a list of 5 students who were ineligible

Civil Service

- Accumulated over 420 volunteer and practical experience hours since the fall of 2003
- **Wentlings Corner Community Club** *(2000–Present)*
- Participated in fundraising activities that totaled over $4,000 per summer
- **Knox Area Baseball League** *(2000–2004)*
- Sold over $1,000 in sponsorships and completed billings to eight local companies

Skills
- Successfully completed a Microsoft Windows training course at Slippery Rock University
  - Proficient in Microsoft Word, Microsoft Excel, and Microsoft PowerPoint
- Competent in Adobe PageMaker and Adobe Photoshop
  - Created and formatted an eight-page program for a fundraiser benefiting Hurricane Katrina victims where over $5,000 was raised

Certifications
- Certified in Emergency Care First Aid until May of 2009
- Certified in Adult and Child CPR until May of 2008
- Certified in Adult and Child AED until May of 2008

References
- **Dr. Catherine Boson**, *Professor of Sport Management*
  Slippery Rock University of Pennsylvania
  12 South Gym, Slippery Rock, PA 16057
  (724)-738-0178   cboson@sru.edu

- **Mr. Josh Kurtz**, *Ticket Office Manager*
  Pittsburgh Steelers
  100 Stadium Avenue, Pittsburgh, PA 15212
  (412)-699-0424   KurtzJ@steelers.nfl.com

- **Mr. Robert Muenster**, *Sports Information Director*
  Clarion University of Pennsylvania
  840 Wood St. Alumni House, Clarion, PA 16214
  (814)-395-2817   rmuenster@clarion.edu

SAMPLE PRINT RÉSUMÉ #2

<u>**William N. Blood**</u>

Current Address	**Home Address**
1220 Stanley Circle	124 N. Bowline Rd.
Naples, FL 34104	Conneautville, PA 16408
239.218.4029	814-545-9986
carcina@fgcu.edu	bblood133sru@yahoo.com

<u>Education</u>

Slippery Rock University   Slippery Rock, PA
B.S. in Sport Management   Anticipated Graduation 2004
Business Administration Minor

<u>Professional Experience</u>

Slippery Rock University Aebersold   Slippery Rock, PA
Recreational Center Building Supervisor   December 2000–Summer 2003

- ➢ Responsible for 10–15 student workers throughout entire facility
- ➢ Accountable for day-to-day operations of entire facility (Intramural Sports, Aerobics/Fitness Programs, S.R.H.S swim practices, Facility Rentals, Student Recreation)
- ➢ Responsible for over 400 participants per shift; dealt with complaints, injuries, conflicts between participants, and enforced rules and regulations of facility
- ➢ Accountable for between $50–$100 of membership money per shift
- ➢ Acted as liaison between student staff, student participants, community members, and professional A.R.C. staff in enforcing facility policies and procedures.

Goo Goo Dolls Gutterflower Tour Concert   Slippery Rock, PA
ARC Building Supervisor   November 10, 2002

- ➢ Responsible for over 35 student volunteers in the operational procedures before, during, and after show (concert set-up, security during show, and tear-down after show)
- ➢ Accountable for troubleshooting before, during, and after show in terms of facility and crowd management; enforce ARC policies to over 2,500 fans
- ➢ Acted as liaison between student volunteers, University Program Board staff, professional ARC staff, stage technicians, professional security staff, and Gutterflower Tour Manager/Crew

The Erie SeaWolves   Erie, PA
Ticket Sales   May 2000–August 2002

- ➢ Prepare and sell all game-day and advance tickets with an emphasis on efficiency, accuracy, and professional customer service
- ➢ Responsible for accurate accounting of money tills (from $300 to $1,000)

Slippery Rock University Aebersold   Slippery Rock, PA
Recreational Center Welcome Center Monitor   December 1999–December 2000

- ➢ Check in from 200 to 500 participants of the recreational facility by means of an ID daily (either student, faculty, staff, or community membership)
- ➢ Check in and out various types of equipment to the facility's members
- ➢ Responsible for completing 10–20 memberships to community members, alumni, families, etc. per day
- ➢ Responsible for over $200 per day in membership and merchandise money

Practicum Experience
Slippery Rock University Aebersold   Slippery Rock, PA
Recreation Center Practicum Student   Fall 2002
- ➤ Designed 5 ARC promotional table tents to be distributed in dining halls (contained dates of Intramural Sports, Aerobics/Fitness Programs, Outdoor Adventures Programs, and other pertinent information concerning ARC programs)
- ➤ Assisted Director of Campus Recreation in updating the ARC website
- ➤ Assisted Intramural Department in scheduling referees
- ➤ Designed over 10 promotional flyers and brochures concerning ARC programs and policies/procedures

Awards
- ➤ Pennsylvania State House of Representatives   Winter 2001
  Certificate of Heroism

References

Gregory Szosa   Dr. Catherine Boson
Director of Campus Recreation   Sport Management Professor
Slippery Rock University   Slippery Rock University
Fraternity Advisor   Student Advisor/Professor
724.712.9909   724.712.1255
gregory.szosa@sru.edu   cboson@sru.edu

Karen Searle   Matt Ordinal
Assistant Director of Campus Recreation   Assistant General Manager
Slippery Rock University   Erie SeaWolves (AA affiliate)
Supervisor at ARC   Friend/Supervisor
724.612.2436   800.123.8878
karen.searle@sru.edu   mattb@seawolves.com

Others available upon request

SAMPLE PRINT RÉSUMÉ #3

Christy Clementi

1100 Rexall Street
Albion, NY 13302
(315) 442-2501
christinaclementi@inkmail.com

Education

SUNY Oswego
Bachelor of Science Degree in Sport Management

Practical Experience in Sport

- **Precision Fitness Center** *(May 2009–August 2009)*
  - Worked with management and sales staff as a full-time intern
  - Supervised patient scheduling and correspondence for the adjoining chiropractic center, Highlands Chiropractic
  - Marketed facility events, including the annual golf scramble and 10K race
  - Generated over $1,500 in donations for the annual golf scramble
- **Oswego Athletic Department** *(January 2008–May 2009)*
  - Assisted in the setup and tear-down of the facility on 12 game days
  - Coordinated halftime promotions for 12 men's and women's basketball games
  - Contacted 36 local businesses to obtain prizes for the winners of the halftime promotions
  - Created and distributed 125 flyers in support of upcoming games
  - Supervised three student workers at the concession stand during the 2009 baseball season
- **Somerset Area Hockey Association** *(May 2007–August 2007)*
  - Organized, created, and formatted a 15-page media guide for three hockey teams
  - Contacted local businesses to obtain sponsorships for the media guide
  - Developed and maintained a database including over 30 parents, players, and coaches

Civil Service

Accumulated over 350 volunteer and practical experience hours since the fall of 2005
- **"Evening in the Endzone" Banquet** *(January 2008–May 2008)*
  - Chair of the organizational committee
  - Coordinated transportation for 25 students attending the banquet
  - Gathered $300 in sponsorships
- **Oswego Minor Hockey** *(June 2007–August 2007)*
  - Assisted sales staff in renewing over $500 in corporate sponsorships for the 2007–2008 hockey season
  - Created an Excel database and recorded all sponsorship information
- **Somerset Area Hockey Association** *(2000–2008)*
  - Assisted team president in arranging bus transportation for 35 student-athletes
  - Assisted team treasurer in fundraising events, creating Treasurer's Reports, and managing 20 student accounts

Ancillary Experience

- **Nike Factory Store** *(August 2007–February 2009)*
  - Cash register operator—responsible for $3,500 per shift
  - Top sales person in the apparel and footwear departments for two months

Skills & Certifications
- Certified in adult and infant CPR, first aid, and AED
- Proficient in Microsoft Word, Excel, PowerPoint, Publisher, and FrontPage
- Three years' experience with Microsoft FrontPage and HTML

References
- **Dr. Roger Williams**, *Chair, Department of Sport Management*
  SUNY Oswego
  224 West Gym, Oswego, NY 13302
  (315) 738-2967   roger.williams@sunyoswego.edu

- **Dr. Benjamin Crow**, *Associate Professor, Sport Management*
  SUNY Brockport
  227 Memorial Center, Brockport, NY 14420
  (585) 832-2392   b.crow@sunybrockport.edu

- **Mr. George Grove**, *General Manager and Exercise Physiologist*
  Precision Fitness Center
  201 Georgian Place, Albion, NY 13302
  (315) 443-3230   george@myprecisionfitness.com

SAMPLE PRINT RÉSUMÉ #4

Rebecca Mansfield
Rebecca.mansfield@gmail.com

Campus Address   **Permanent Address**
859 Wine Rd   3132 Moss Drive
Annapolis, MD 21401   Crownsville, MD 21032
(410) 362-5628   (410) 423-3538

EDUCATION
St. John's College
Bachelor of Science Degree in Sport Management   Minor in Spanish
Graduation *May 2009*   GPA: 3.87

PRACTICAL AND WORK EXPERIENCE
Anne Arundel County Parks & Recreation Camp Counselor, Annapolis, MD   *Summer 2008*
- Supervised recreational activities for 65 day camp children over six weeks
- Monitored the environment for children with medical problems and was responsible for administering medications as needed
- Created and organized alternate activities during inclement weather

Campus Recreation, St John's College   *Spring 2008*
- Assisted in facilitation of a basketball tournament by setting up and cleaning up the event, as well as supervising the referees and ensuring the tournament games stayed on schedule
- Assisted with the registration and scoring of the Boulder Bash, a bouldering competition, with approximately 50 participants

ASG Sports, Inc., Baltimore, MD   *Summer 2007*
- Assisted in the registration of six Chick-fil-A soccer clinics with approximately 150 participants each and the Beach Soccer tournament with over 1,200 participants
- Generated schedules for each of the 175 participating in the Beach Soccer tournament
- Created four one-page press releases for the Chick-fil-A soccer clinics, Beach Lacrosse, Beach Soccer and the Chick-fil-A soccer tournament
- Customized event sheets for six events varying from the Ravens Family Picnic to the Mid-Atlantic Sports Network (MASN) events with the Washington Nationals

Rebecca Mansfield   **Page 2**

CIVIL SERVICE

<u>On-Campus Volunteer Experiences,</u> St. John's College, Annapolis, MD

- 5th Annual Steel City Slam Quad Rugby Tournament   *2007*
- World Languages Competition   *2006–2007*
- Note taking for Students with Disabilities   *2005–2007*
- Special Olympics   *2005–2007*

PROFESSIONAL DEVELOPMENT

- <u>Gamma Sigma Sigma Service Sorority</u>   *2007–2008*
  - o   Gamma Sigma Sigma is a service organization that works with groups such as Special Olympics, Habitat for Humanity, and Alex's Lemonade Stand. In 2008, I was elected the financial secretary. I was responsible for collecting dues and the money that was raised for service organizations.
- <u>North American Society for Sport Managers</u>   *2007–2008*
  - o   I am a student member of NASSM, which is an organization that actively seeks to enhance and support professionals in the field of sport, recreation, or leisure.
- <u>Placed 2nd in the Sport Marketing Association Case Study</u> Competition   *2007*
  - o   I was invited to be a member of a four-person team that participated in the case study competition section of the SMA conference. Our team was given a problem and, in four hours, asked to create a presentation with a solution to this problem. Our team placed 2nd in the competition.
- <u>Stadium Manager's Association</u>   *2007*
  - o   I am a student member of SMA, which promotes management of stadiums around the world.
- <u>Attended Sport Management Trips to Costa Rica (2006) and Ireland (2007)</u>   *2006–2007*
  - o   I attended two trips with the sport management department. In 2006, we visited Costa Rica and, in 2007, we visited Ireland. In Costa Rica, we visited the Rawlings baseball factory and listened to presentations about soccer and baseball. In Ireland, we visited Croke Park and the K Club. These trips gave me a better understanding of sport management in an international light.

REFERENCES

Dr. Debbie Glenn	*Ms. Sally Jensen*	*Mr. Tim Nimet*
University of Maryland	Baltimore Blast	Gold's Gym
140 Century Hall	1301 South Ellwood Ave	8444 Greenbelt Rd
College Park, MD 20742	Baltimore, MD 21224	Greenbelt, MD 20770
301-738-2788	410-482-4254	301-208-0076
Debrah.glenn@umd.edu	sjensen@baltimoreblast.com	pumpup@zoominternet.net

SAMPLE PRINT RÉSUMÉ # 5

Laura Pimentel

Phone: (818) 988-8484
Address: 2400 N. Chestnut #12, Fresno, CA 93710
Email: pimentel22z@yahoo.com
Website: http://laurapimentel.webs.com

Education

California State University, Fresno
Bachelor of Science Degree in Recreation Administration
Emphasis in Sports and Entertainment Facility Management

Professional Experience

- **Fresno Grizzlies** *(December 2008 to Present)*
  - o Sold over $50,000 for the upcoming 2010 season
  - o Completed $80,470 worth of ticket sales during the 2009 season
  - o Serviced 15 corporate sponsor accounts worth $360,000 of sponsor revenue
  - o Assisted with Making The Grade program, which raises over $10,000 each year
  - o Serviced over 60 season ticket clients daily by phone and e-mail

- **Fresno Grizzlies** *(May 2008 to November 2008)*
  - o Counted money produced in Fun Zone area, averaging about $830/night
  - o Created work schedules for 150 game day staff
  - o Assisted Director of Event Operations in managing 150 game day staff
  - o Completed daily labor reports of 150 game day staff following each game

- **Direct File** *(April 2007 to May 2008)*
  - o Created monthly e-newsletters that were sent to over 100 people
  - o Produced bulk mailings every other month with over 300 mailings
  - o Reconciled bank accounts weekly for 10 clients

Other Experience

- Delta Zeta Valley Diamonds *(February 2008 to Present)*
  - o Helped in establishing local alumnae group in Fresno, CA
  - o Created website for alumnae group and continue to update
  - o Received "Most Outstanding Website" Award in the Western Area from Delta Zeta National Headquarters

- Delta Zeta National Sorority *(2003 to 2007)*
  - o Created & managed budgets for all eight executive officers
  - o Conducted weekly meetings with organized agendas
  - o Managed eight executive board members and entire sorority of 40 women
  - o Deposited all monies, totaling an average of $500/month

Affiliations

- Fresno Women's Network *(April 2009 to Present)*
  - o Attend Membership Committee meetings, member of Website Committee; attend most monthly luncheons and networking events

- Stadium Managers Association *(2008)*
  - o Attended 37th Annual Stadium Managers Association seminar in San Diego, CA *(2008)*

Skills

- Competent in Adobe Photoshop
  - o Produced over 25 flyers used in various events at the Fresno Grizzlies
- Proficient in Microsoft Word, Microsoft Excel, Microsoft PowerPoint, and Microsoft Outlook

References

- **Garrett Fahrmann**, *Senior Vice President of Operations*
  Fresno Grizzlies
  1800 Tulare Street, Fresno, CA 93721
  (571) 213-1789
  fahrmagr@hotmail.com

- **Jason Hannold**, Director of Tickets
  Fresno Grizzlies
  1800 Tulare Street, Fresno, CA 93721
  (724) 556-9430
  jhannold@fresnogrizzlies.com

- **Jennifer Frankito**, *Vice President of Operations*
  Direct File
  504 Van Ness Ave., Fresno, CA 93721
  (559) 285-9747
  jfrankito@directfile.com

Application

Now that you have seen some good examples of print résumés, let's look at two that contain errors and omissions. Applications 5.2 and 5.3 provide practice in identifying errors and omissions in print résumés. These Applications are identical to the cover letter Applications you completed in chapter 4. At this point, test your understanding of résumés by circling the errors and missing information. Then check your answers against the errors and omissions we identified.

Application 5.2: Résumé Corrections Application

Nita A. Job

3690 E Mohican St Apt 3423
Aurora, IL 60504
(630) 246-4430
E-mail: njob37@yahoo.com

===========================Work Experience===========================

NBC – Live Nation LLC.
Aurora, IL: March 15, 2006–Present

Operations Manager
- Organize and Coordinate the Operations and Site Construction for the Dew Action Sports Tour
- The primary contact for all vendors and other divisions on-site
- Manage an on-site crew of 15–25 operations and event services staff
- Manage and oversee the operational budget for the entire tour
- Negotiate and manage all national and local vendors
- Create the Production and Front of House Rider for each venue
- Oversee and relay all duties of each Venue Manager

Clear Channel Entertainment—Motor Sports (Live Nation Motor Sports)
Aurora, IL: December 12, 2003–March 15, 2006

CCE-Motor Sports Event Manager
- Set Up and Direct 28 Monster Jam-or-Thunder Nationals Events
- 10,000–25,000 spectators attended each event on average
- Balanced event budgets that ranged from $ 38,000–$95,000
- Miscellaneous duties such as
  - Pro Truck Contingency Program Manager
  - Training of the New Event Managers
  - Communications Manager for all 4 wheel properties

Venue Manager for the Dew Action Sports Tour (June 2005–October 2005)
- Set Up and Coordinate all aspects of the Dirt Venue at the Dew Action Sports Tour
- Sponsorship implementation in each venue for Live Television on NBC and USA
- Manage 3–5 local staff during construction and move-out of venue
- Work hand in hand with Television director on Camera Placement
  - Aided in 19 day tour set up to tear down each stop
  - Directed offsite Freestyle Motocross Promotions

Operations Manager for the Toyota AMA Arenacross Series (October 2005–March 2005)
- Set up and Direct 13 Toyota AMA Regional Arenacross Events
- Oversee 10 Toyota AMA National Arenacross Events and Staff
- Sponsor Implementation with both National and Regional Series
- Manage all back and front of house budget numbers for each event and overall series
  - Handled all media relations and distribution
  - Coordinated final banquet for entire tour
  - Train new event managers for various Live Nation properties

Grove City YMCA Grove City, PA: September 2001–September 2003
    Building Supervisor/ Referee
- Supervision of entire recreation facility
- Supervision of 50–100 school age children
- Refereeing Volleyball

Assistant Fitness Specialist/ Customer Service Manager
- Aided in knowledge of all around fitness and machinery to over 2,500 club members
- Designed membership plans and assisted in sales and marketing of the club
- Dealt with one on one interaction with over fifteen potential members per day

==============================**Education**==============================
Slippery Rock University, Fall 1999–Spring 2004
Major: Sport Management/ specialization in Sport Fitness/Business
Minor: Business Administration
==============================**References**==============================
Available Upon Request

Answers to 5.2

Nita A. Job

3690 E Mohican St Apt 3423
Aurora, IL 60504
(630) 246-4430
E-mail: njob37@yahoo.com

Change to RELEVANT WORK EXPERIENCE

===========================**Work Experience**===========================

NBC – Live Nation LLC.

Aurora, IL: March 15, 2006–Present

Operations Manager

- Organize and Coordinate the Operations and Site Construction for the Dew Action Sports Tour This is a duty… it needs to be changed into an accomplishment (quantify it)
- The primary contact for all vendors and other divisions on-site
- Manage an on-site crew of 15–25 operations and event services staff
- Manage and oversee the operational budget for the entire tour
- Negotiate and manage all national and local vendors
- Create the Production and Front of House Rider for each venue
- Oversee and relay all duties of each Venue Manager

These don't say what the applicant did; they need to be quantified (made "measurable").

Clear Channel Entertainment—Motor Sports (Live Nation Motor Sports)
Aurora, IL: December 12, 2003–March 15, 2006

CCE-Motor Sports Event Manager

- Set Up and Direct 28 Monster Jam-or-Thunder Nationals Events
- 10,000–25,000 spectators attended each event on average
- Balanced event budgets that ranged from $ 38,000–$95,000
- Miscellaneous duties such as
  - Pro Truck Contingency Program Manager
  - Training of the New Event Managers
  - Communications Manager for all 4 wheel properties

All of these are "Duties," not an accomplishment; student even uses the word

Venue Manager for the Dew Action Sports Tour (June 2005–October 2005)

- Set Up and Coordinate all aspects of the Dirt Venue at the Dew Action Sports Tour
- Sponsorship implementation in each venue for Live Television on NBC and USA
- Manage 3–5 local staff during construction and move-out of venue
- Work hand in hand with Television director on Camera Placement
  - Aided in 19 day tour set up to tear down each stop
  - Directed offsite Freestyle Motocross Promotions

If you are currently employed the verb tenses should be present otherwise all verb tenses must be in the past tense!! Every blurb must begin with an action verb.

Operations Manager for the Toyota AMA Arenacross Series (October 2005–March 2005)
- Set up and Direct 13 Toyota AMA Regional Arenacross Events
- Oversee 10 Toyota AMA National Arenacross Events and Staff
- Sponsor Implementation with both National and Regional Series
- Manage all back and front of house budget numbers for each event and overall series
  - Handled all media relations and distribution
  - Coordinated final banquet for entire tour
  - Train new event managers for various Live Nation properties

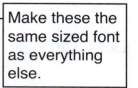
Should be March – October

Make these the same sized font as everything else.

Grove City YMCA Grove City, PA: September 2001–September 2003
    Building Supervisor/ Referee
- Supervision of entire recreation facility
- Supervision of 50–100 school age children
- Refereeing Volleyball

These need to be "quantified." Make them into accomplishment statements.

Assistant Fitness Specialist/ Customer Service Manager
- Aided in knowledge of all around fitness and machinery to over 2,500 club members
- Designed membership plans and assisted in sales and marketing of the club
- Dealt with one on one interaction with over fifteen potential members per day

===============================**Education**==============================
Slippery Rock University, Fall 1999–Spring 2004
Major: Sport Management/ specialization in Sport Fitness/Business
Minor: Business Administration

===============================**References**=============================
Available Upon Request

Always put down your references! It could be the difference between getting a job and not getting one. Use 3 in the following format:
Name
Title
Organization
Organization address
Organization phone
City, State Zip
Email address

Application 5.3: Résumé Corrections Application

Lisa Marie Pratt

3894 West Liberty Avenue #1
Pittsburgh, Pennsylvania 15216
Phone: 724.421.7630   Email: lmpratt@yahoo.com

Career Objective:
- Undergraduate degree Sport Management – Spring 2006
- Undergraduate degree Marketing – Spring 2007
- Undergraduate degree Business Management – Spring 2007
- Masters degree Sport Management – Begin Fall 2007

Practical Experiences:
>   Beaver Valley YMCA - Beaver, PA
>   Herron Recreation and Fitness Center - California, PA
>   California University Club Sports - California, PA
>>   *Skills acquired through practicums*: Facility Management, Planning and Organizing, Supervising, Microsoft Office programs, CLASS, Front Desk Work, Development of documents such as constitutions and by-laws, Time management

Education:
>   **College:**
>>   California University of Pennsylvania
>>   California, PA
>>   Sport Management – senior – 3.6
>>   Expected date of graduation – May 2006

>   **Conferences:**
>>   Presented at the Robert Morris Sport Management conference 2004.

Work History:
>   02/04 - Present: **Herron Recreation and Fitness Center**
>>   Position: Building Supervisor
>>   Supervisor:
>>   Kris Powell (Assistant Director of Campus Recreation) – (724) 938-8375
>>   California, PA 15419

Community Services:

   * Care Break in Baltimore, MD during spring break 2005 – 168 hours of service
   * Habitat for Humanity   * Take a Kid to the Game
   * Senior Care Day   * Hoops for Hunger
   * Relay for Life   * CSC Event Staff
   * Tree planting in Alleghany National Forest

References Available Upon Request

Answers to 5.3

Lisa Marie Pratt

3894 West Liberty Avenue #1
Pittsburgh, Pennsylvania 15216
Phone: 724.421.7630   Email: lmpratt@yahoo.com

Too much "dead" space. The heading needs better balance.

Career Objective:

HOW are these objectives? For that matter why do you need an objective? Isn't the objective of a résumé to get an interview?

- Undergraduate degree Sport Management – Spring 2006
- Undergraduate degree Marketing – Spring 2007
- Undergraduate degree Business Management – Spring 2007
- Masters degree Sport Management – Begin Fall 2007

Practical Experiences:

"Related Work Exp." would be a better descriptor.

Beaver Valley YMCA - Beaver, PA
Herron Recreation and Fitness Center - California, PA
California University Club Sports - California, PA

Skills acquired through practicums: Facility Management, Planning and Organizing, Supervising, Microsoft Office programs, CLASS, Front Desk Work, Development of documents such as constitutions and by-laws, Time management

Education:

College:

These are "duties." They need to be quantified—in other words, attach numbers to them.

California University of Pennsylvania
California, PA
Sport Management – senior – 3.6
Expected date of graduation – May 2006

What is this? Do not assume that the reader will know what you are talking about.

Conferences:

Presented at the Robert Morris Sport Management conference 2004.

Work History:

What did you present on? How is this significant? Again, do not assume.

02/04 - Present: **Herron Recreation and Fitness Center**
Position: Building Supervisor
Supervisor:

What did you do?

Kris Powell (Assistant Director of Campus Recreation) – (724) 938-8375
California, PA 15419

Community Services:

* Care Break in Baltimore, MD during spring break 2005 – 168 hours of service
* Habitat for Humanity   * Take a Kid to the Game
* Senior Care Day   * Hoops for Hunger
* Relay for Life   * CSC Event Staff
* Tree planting in Alleghany National Forest

Relevance? What skills were developed while involved with these experiences?

References Available Upon Request

Always include at least three references.

Electronic and Scannable Résumés

Due to the large number of résumés they receive, some sport agencies have begun to request electronic or *scannable* résumés. Scannable résumés are print résumés constructed to ensure efficient and accurate processing by scanners. Although electronic and scannable résumés are different types of résumés, the content and format of these two résumés are essentially identical. However, it is important to understand the differences between a traditional print and electronic or scannable résumé. We recommend that you construct and keep an updated electronic and scannable print résumé on hand, in case the need for one arises.

In most cases the content of the electronic or scannable résumé is very similar to the content of a traditional print résumé, but there are a couple of notable differences. One major difference is that electronic and scannable résumés should emphasize profession-related nouns, or "keywords" rather than "action verbs." This is important because electronic and scannable résumés are scanned, using keyword or key phrase searches, to select applicants who have specific skills that the employer is seeking. If these skills (i.e., as expressed in keywords, key phrases) do not appear on your electronic or scannable résumé, you will not be selected for further consideration. A second difference is that electronic and scannable résumés generally include a brief summary in which the applicant highlights the professional skills he or she possesses. This summary should include the keywords or phrases that indicate you have the skills that are most important for the position vacancy. A well-constructed summary also increases the chances of your electronic or scannable résumé being selected for further consideration by a prospective employer.

The major differences between a traditional print and electronic or scannable résumé relate to format. Because electronic and scannable résumés are usually scanned by machine prior to selection, the way information is presented is of paramount importance. It is *essential* to structure the résumé so that it is easily and accurately scanned for content. The following formatting tips will help you prepare your electronic or scannable résumé:

- Save your electronic or scannable résumé as plain text (.txt), Portable Document Format (.pdf), or Rich Text Format (.rtf). This will ensure that your résumé is readable by a wide variety of word processing applications and computer platforms. It also protects against transmitting a virus with your résumé.
- Do not use graphics, lines, shading, boxes, bullets, or other such features that might interfere with accurate scanning (dashes are usually effective alternatives to bullets).
- Avoid using italics, bold, or underlines (use uppercase to distinguish headings).
- Limit the amount of words, and ensure that there is plenty of white space to avoid errors during scanning.
- Avoid abbreviations, unless universally used and accepted (e.g., state abbreviations, such as CA).
- Place telephone area codes within parentheses to ensure recognition by scanners.
- Begin entries on the left margin and avoid unconventional formatting, such as multiple columns. If you choose to indent or center something, it must be done by repeatedly pressing the spacebar. Do not use the tab key or centering option.
- For scannable print résumés, use clear, plain fonts such as Arial, Times, or Helvetica. For size of font, use 11 to 12 points.
- If sending hard copies for scanning, send only originals, mail in a large envelope to avoid folding the résumé, and do not staple two-page résumés.

Web Résumés

In addition to developing traditional print and electronic or scannable résumés, you may want to prepare a résumé for posting on the Web. There are now many tools to help you create a résumé web page, such as Adobe's Dreamweaver. These software packages make creating an attractive web page relatively easy. If you have a Macintosh and are a subscriber to MobileMe (formerly .mac) and have the iLife suite of tools on your computer, you can use the new iWeb software with the résumé template to put your résumé together. If you know HTML (hypertext markup language), you can build your own web page using any text editor. More-over, many word processor applications now offer .html as one of the file formats to which you can save a document. This means you can build your résumé in Microsoft Word and then save it in the HTML format. Then, upload your HTML résumé to your web server and your web résumé is ready for viewing by anyone who has your web address (URL). If you decide to use a web résumé, remember to update it regularly and be sure to include its URL on your business card and professional correspondence. Many campuses provide web space to their students. Check with your student computing resources to see if your campus provides this.

Portfolios

A portfolio normally includes a variety of documents. Think of a portfolio as a large file that contains an ac-cumulation of personal information. Items such as illustrations of sport-specific projects, evidence of member-ship in professional organizations, certifications, a current résumé, examples of any unique skills (such as web design), and other important documents all become part of your personal portfolio. While there are two main styles of portfolio, we will concentrate on the "professional" portfolio.

Normally when reviewing a traditional résumé, the potential employer assesses the majority of the infor-mation contained in the résumé. However, during an interview the format may not allow every item on the résumé to be discussed with the potential employer, and sometimes additional experiences have been acquired by the applicant after the résumé was initially submitted. An alternative strategy is to bring selected items in a small interview portfolio with you to the interview. An interview portfolio provides you with several im-portant benefits. First, an interview portfolio will not only provide an update to your résumé, it allows you to present examples of your best work in a convenient and professional manner. These examples can attest to your writing skills, organizational abilities, technological skills, and professional expertise. The more skills you can demonstrate through your portfolio, the more valuable you will be to a potential internship site. For example, a portfolio can allow you to demonstrate proficiency in a wide variety of computer software, such as PowerPoint, Excel, FileMaker Pro, iMovie, Photoshop, etc. Second, the amount of work required to prepare a quality interview portfolio will demonstrate to the potential employer your desire for the position. Finally, very few applicants for sport management positions possess an interview portfolio. Presenting one during an interview will set you apart from the other candidates you are competing against.

Tips on Compiling an Interview Portfolio

1. Put your information in a 1–2-inch binder—use a colorful cover page.
2. Do not use plastic page protectors.
3. Use copies of all your material. Never provide the "official" copy.
4. Use index tabs and a title page to divide each section. Provide a summary page at the beginning of each section.
5. Use consistent headings for samples of any coursework.
6. Arrange your sections so they correspond to the information contained in the job description.
7. Absolutely, positively ensure that the portfolio looks professional and error free; this applies to grammar, punctuation and spelling!
8. The information in your portfolio needs to be up-to-date and representative of your best work. We suggest updating your portfolio every six months to one year.

Presentation Format

1. Cover page (your name, address, phone and cell number, e-mail, possible graphic)
2. Typed letter of introduction (similar to a cover letter with no address)
3. Typed résumé (on professional paper)

4. Two to three letters of recommendation

5. Reflection Statement (optional)—This is a "self-assessment" of where are you at this time in your life. Include both your strengths and weaknesses. This section needs a LOT of thought before writing it.

6. Three samples of sport-specific work—business plans, budgets, marketing plans, and research projects can be effectively highlighted in a portfolio.

7. A copy of your college transcripts (optional)

8. A brief discussion about your practical and volunteer experiences

9. Examples of skills or certifications (First Aid/CPR; web design; fluency in another language, etc.)

10. Evidence of membership in professional organizations or even conferences you have attended.

Electronic Portfolio

An electronic portfolio may be used instead and should include most of the above components. This style of portfolio has the advantage of using sophisticated features (e.g., audio, video, interactive elements) to emphasize your professional assets and capabilities. If you use a web-based portfolio, be sure to include your site's address (URL) on your résumé. If you elect to construct an electronic portfolio, a digital recorder should be one of your tools. The recorder can be used for documenting events, projects, and other items that could be included in a web-based or CD-ROM portfolio. Begin now to establish an ongoing, visual record of your professional involvement.

Video Résumés

YouTube video clips are extremely popular, and beginning in 2006 they spawned the advent of *video résumés*. By 2007 over 4,000 were available. A video résumé allows an individual the opportunity to demonstrate certain characteristics, such as personality, that a textual résumé cannot. Seeing the candidate and viewing their presentation provides a potential employer with a unique perspective. However, not everyone is in favor of new gadgets, so caution needs to be used before embracing the concept. While some individuals don't believe a video résumé would play an important role in hiring decisions, others are very interested in the technological possibilities. A 2007 survey found that 17% of the respondents had watched video résumés, but 89% said they would watch if they were made available (*USA Today,* April 25, 2007, B-3). Creating these video résumés is not very intimidating. In fact all that is needed is a PC-mounted web camera (less than $100.00) and movie maker software (Microsoft Windows XP provides one for free). However, since quality is paramount, you might wish to have a professional create your video résumé. Start-up companies currently exist to fill the niche, but they don't come cheap. While a video résumé will definitely set you apart from the overwhelming number of résumés received by a sport business, the investment of time and resources for a video résumé will be much more extensive than with a traditional version. You need to decide if the potential benefits are worth the possible risks.

Summary

Chapters 4 and 5 have provided you with suggestions and various examples of quality cover letters and résumés. You now possess two powerful tools in your search for a quality internship. It would be easy to take one of our examples and replace the current information with your own data. However, that could prove damaging to your future with a sport agency. A résumé is your tool and should be a reflection of you and your strengths. Not everyone looks the same and not all résumés should look similar either. Develop the tool that will work best for you. This process requires a commitment of time and effort on your part. However, this effort is an investment in your future. Surprisingly enough, some individuals spend less time on résumé preparation on a daily basis than they do in texting their friends—how many of their friends do you think will get them a job?

Developing your résumé and cover is now completed. Therefore, it is time to prepare you for the "big" day. Interviewing is a skill, and similar to learning to dribble with your left hand, interview strategy must be learned and then practiced over and over. We will provide you with the appropriate tactics… it will be up to you to practice.

Chapter Six
The Interview

Ability is what you are capable of doing; motivation determines what you do.
Attitude determines how you will do it.

---Lou Holtz---

You have now prepared a quality cover letter and résumé, but if you haven't prepared yourself for the interview, all your hard work can be undone very easily. Your game plan for success can ill afford any mistakes at this stage. The importance of taking the time to properly plan for an interview can not be overstated. Most of you will have minimal experience with interviews, so this chapter will describe the process as well as provide some specific strategies that will increase your chances of a successful interview. The day of the interview looms large, so let's get started.

Preparing for an Interview

Developing the Proper Frame of Mind

CONFIDENCE! This is the overriding mindset that you must exude throughout the interview. You notice that we said "confidence." Oftentimes students get to the interview stage and feel almost undeserving when an organization grants them an interview. All the academic work, the practical experiences, and the volunteer service you have accomplished, though, have created an individual who is a valuable commodity. All too often potential interns overlook these attributes. Of course you need to stay grounded and not appear too brash.

As you approach the big day, it is important to understand that an internship interview is a two-way process. You are, of course, being evaluated by the interviewer, but you are also evaluating whether this agency and agency supervisor are right for you. Recognizing that you are an equal participant in the interview process is essential—it will help give you confidence and ensure that you are in the proper frame of mind throughout the interview. Moreover, research has shown that many interviewers do not take the time to prepare properly for their interviews. If you have thoroughly prepared for your half of the interview, you will often have the advantage in an interview situation. The foundation of a successful interview is to think positively and project a confident, professional image.

Doing Your Homework

Let's reflect on the new house that we have been constructing. We have selected the site, we have designed the house, and we have built it. Now it is time to "sell" the house. Obviously the house we are preparing to sell is ourself. By constructing and implementing our game plan for success we have been able to select an internship site, we have designed and sent out our cover letter and résumé, and now we are preparing to go out and convince a potential internship representative that we are their best choice for the position. Planning and preparation have been of paramount importance up to this point and the interview is no different. We researched the organization and now we need to plan for the actual interview.

Logistical Concerns

Numerous obstacles crop up while preparing for the interview and many of them, while they appear trivial, can determine your success or failure. You must be able to travel from point A to point B. Sometimes this is not as easy as it sounds. Being unfamiliar with the surroundings, traffic congestion, and/or road construction have caused many interview plans to go awry. Technology such as a GPS device or On-Star can make a difficult situation very manageable. Other minute details such as what to wear, knowing where to park, and having an extra copy or two of your résumé are critical to proper preparation. A professional attitude and attention to detail will help to ensure that the interviewer's first impression is a positive one. The phrase we previously discussed, "proper planning prevents poor performance," becomes very relevant at this point of the interview process.

The interview process can be a very stressful one, and due to a heightened sense of anxiety we sometimes forget even the simplest detail. For example, having your cell phone begin ringing during the interview is not a good idea. Putting it on vibrate is a simple task that might be overlooked in the midst of rushing around before the interview. The following six items should be implemented during the interview process. They will help to provide some organization during this stressful time.

1. *Confirmation Letter or Call.* We all make mistakes, but showing up for an interview on the wrong day or at the wrong time can prove to be a "deal breaker." You probably own a cell phone... be proactive and call to confirm the date, time, and location a day or two before the event. You can also use this call to your advantage by asking about the proper exit from the interstate, parking instructions, and the correct side of the building to enter.

2. *Trial Run.* There is a definite reason why scientists go through multiple tests before unveiling a new product. They want to make sure all the kinks have been alleviated before making it public. You should use a similar technique a day or two before your interview. You should verify you know the best route to take, while at the same time anticipating time of day, traffic patterns, etc. Be sure you pay attention to how long it takes as well taking into account the previously mentioned details. The traffic congestion on a Sunday afternoon will not be the same as on Monday morning at 8:00 a.m. as you try to navigate rush-hour traffic on your way to the interview location. Be sure to practice an alternative route.

3. *Your Portfolio.* If you have a print portfolio, you should consider taking it to the interview with you. You might offer your portfolio during the interview or even at the end of the interview; however, do *not* force the portfolio on the interviewer. Let him or her know that it exists and be ready to show it with pride. If you have developed a web-based portfolio, let the interviewer know about it and be sure to provide him or her with the URL for your portfolio. Return to the end of chapter 5 ("The Résumé") for additional details about the portfolio.

4. *Review of Agency Data.* In chapter 3 ("Search and Research"), we emphasized the importance of doing extensive research on various sport-management organizations. Some of these you became interested in and others you jettisoned. A day or two before the interview is the time to review this information. Also, additional, more recent information may now be available. An interviewer will be impressed if you demonstrate knowledge about his or her agency.

5. *Self-Assessment Review.* We have discussed the importance of your game plan for success. The applications we provided to you in chapter 1 ("Self-Assessment") were designed to assist in the creation of your game plan which is intended to help you to understand yourself more thoroughly. The interview is the first step in your game plan and is the gateway to your first full-time position. During an interview the interviewer will attempt to discover if you understand yourself and your own capabilities. A properly designed game plan will ensure your understanding of these qualities and reviewing the forms in chapter 1 will enhance your preparation.

6. *Anticipating the Questions.* You can prepare for interview questions. Put yourself in the place of the interviewer (you may have their position in a year or two!). What kinds of information would you deem relevant for the position? In addition, utilize your networks. Ask your professors the types of questions you could expect. Ask other classmates. Some of them may have interviewed for similar positions. Finally, contact some of your school's alumni. They may work in the same field, have interviewed for a similar position, or be savvy enough to provide quality suggestions. In case a question arises, be certain that you understand the expectations of your university's sport management program. Familiarize yourself with this information because, even if a question doesn't occur during the interview, you will probably be asked about it at some point in the process.

Types of Internship Questions

In most cases, an interviewer's questions can be categorized as one of three types: open, probing, or closed. Depending on the type of question asked the interviewer is looking for a specific type of response.

Open-Ended

These types of questions are quite broad in scope and allow flexibility in the candidate's response. A lot of times they will be asked at the very beginning of the interview. While the interviewer is looking for some basic information, the question also helps the interviewer relax. A question such as "please tell me a little bit about yourself" is a prime example of an "open-ended" question. It will provide the interviewer with some information to assess, but will also allow the interviewee a chance to become comfortable while speaking about themselves. There really isn't a time limit for this type of question, but an adequate response would be between one to two minutes.

Probing

A "probing" question is completely different than an open-ended one. Normally, a probing question will be asked for one of two reasons. First, the interviewer has heard some valuable information that he or she deems important and wants further clarification. Second, the interviewee has said something that concerns the interviewer, and before an assessment is made the interviewer wants additional information. An example of a probing question would be, "Please explain why you have only stayed at your previous two positions for six months each?" The response to a probing question should be several sentences in length, but by no means should it be as broad as that for an open-ended question.

Closed-Ended

A "closed-ended" question can usually be answered with a "yes" or "no" response. The interviewer is looking for factual data. At the most it requires a one-sentence reply. The interviewee needs to be short and sweet. An example of a closed-ended question would be, "Are you willing to relocate?"

Understanding the type of question being asked provides the interviewee with a guide as to what type of response as well as what length of response is expected. This information can prove valuable to the interviewee but requires an understanding of the types of questions.

Application

Application 6.1 provides a list of 30 interview questions frequently asked of potential interns. Be proactive and review these questions. Compose a response for each of them. This preparation will help alleviate a great deal of stress and tension later. Be thorough, but concise. After you have finished writing down your answers, give some thought to "Thought-Provoking Questions You Might Be Asked," "Other Potential Questions," and "Behavioral Questions" listed at the end of Application 6.1.

Application 6.1: Internship Interview Questions

Many organizations ask similar questions. The following is a list of commonly asked questions utilized in many types of interviews. We have provided you with a space to record your answer to each of the questions. We do not advocate that you memorize your responses. However, by preparing yourself and planning for the various types of questions you may develop a sense of confidence. This confidence (not cockiness) will permeate throughout the interview.

1. Describe your short-term and long-term goals. What will you need to do in order to attain them?

_____

_____

_____

2. What will you be doing five years from now?

_____

_____

_____

3. What do you consider to be your greatest strengths and weaknesses?

_____

_____

_____

4. What experiences do you have with people from diverse ethnic and religious backgrounds?

_____

_____

_____

5. If we called one of your references, what would he or she say about you?

_____

_____

_____

6. Define the term *disappointment*.

_____

_____

_____

7. Tell me what you know about our organization.

_____

_____

_____

8. Do you work well under pressure? Provide examples.

_____

_____

_____

9. What is the most important lesson you learned in college that will help you as an intern?

_____

_____

_____

10. Why is an internship with this agency important to you?

_____

_____

_____

11. What is your biggest "turn-off"?

_____

_____

_____

12. Describe a mistake you have made in your life and tell me what you learned from it.

_____

_____

_____

13. When you hear the term success, what is the first idea that pops into your head?

_____

_____

_____

14. What qualities do you want your internship supervisor to possess?

_____

_____

_____

15. What is the most important quality a good intern should have?

_____

_____

_____

16. How do you stay up-to-date with the trends in sport management?

_____

_____

_____

17. Describe a problem that you have faced and tell me how you solved it. What would you do differently the next time you are faced with a similar problem?

_____

_____

_____

18. How well do you write?

_____

_____

_____

19. Why do you feel you are qualified for this internship position?

_____

_____

_____

20. What are the three most important things you have learned during college?

_____

_____

_____

21. After doing research into this internship, give me one suggestion on how to improve our organization.

_____

_____

_____

22. How important are grades?

_____

_____

_____

23. What makes you happy?

_____

_____

_____

24. How did you select this internship site?

_____

_____

_____

25. How would you rate your oral speaking skills? What types of groups have you spoken to?

_____

_____

_____

26. What do you find most satisfying in a job?

_____

_____

_____

27. How would you rate your computer skills?

_____

_____

_____

28. What makes someone an ethical person?

_____

_____

_____

29. Tell me about a situation when something that you planned went completely wrong, and what you did to rectify the situation.

_____

_____

_____

30. What motivates you?

_____

_____

_____

Thought-Provoking Questions You Might Be Asked

The ability to be creative and think on your feet is an important attribute interviewers like to assess. These questions take many forms. It is important to realize that there is no wrong answer. The interviewer is interested to see how you respond and the logic you exhibit in determining your response. Each of these questions was actually asked to some of our students.

- What two questions do you not want me to ask you?
- If you were a famous actor, which actor you would be?
- What part of a salad would you be?
- Tell me how cold it is if it is twice as cold as zero degrees?
- If you were to define yourself as one color, what would it be and why?
- If you could be a superhero, what would you want your superpower(s) to be?
- If you won the "Powerball," whom would you share the money with?

Other Potential Questions

- What are the areas that you need to improve on?
- What does the word "integrity" mean to you?
- How did you select your university?
- If someone else has more experience, better grades, and is willing to make the same sacrifices as you, why should I pick you over him or her?
- Do you have a problem with speaking in front of large crowds of people?
- How do you approach giving advice to someone that is your superior?
- How do you expect to meet the expectations in this internship and produce high-quality work?
- Do you like to travel? Why?

Behavioral Questions

You should also be prepared to answer behavioral questions. These questions attempt to determine how you will react to a situation in the future based on how you reacted in the past. By determining your responses the interviewer can evaluate if you will be a good fit with the organization. While any organization is made up of numerous personalities, the "fit" of new employees is a critical decision. Even at an entry-level position, most organizations invest hundreds of thousands of dollars in training new personnel. If they prove to be a distraction or decide to leave after six months, the organization has wasted a tremendous amount of money and resources. The following are some examples of behavioral questions:

- Tell me about a time when you found yourself in an ethically compromising situation. How did you handle it?
- Explain to me the toughest challenge you have faced while involved in sport management. How were you able to overcome it?
- Give me two examples of times when you considered yourself to be a real "team player." Provide specific evidence to support your belief.
- Do you consider yourself to be a good leader? Give me three examples from your past that support your belief.
- What is your biggest pet peeve with other people? If your supervisor had that characteristic, would you discuss it with him/her?

Preparing Questions You Want to Ask

As mentioned previously, as a sport management major with academic, practical, and volunteer experiences, you are valuable. Similar to the organization not wanting to offer a position to the wrong person, you want to be sure that the organization will provide you with the experience and mentoring that you are looking for. Therefore, the internship interview must be a two-way process. You should not leave the interview without knowing the answers to the following questions:

- Who will be your direct supervisor? Has your direct supervisor had experience supervising interns?
- Has the agency had interns before? How often?
- What is the placement rate for previous interns at the agency? Are any of them still employed?
- What hours will you be expected to work? How many hours a week? Will "overtime" be expected?
- What will be your primary duties and responsibilities?
- How much training will you receive at the beginning of the internship?
- Do interns receive any type of compensation?
- Will the agency assist with securing a place to live (only if needed)?
- What type of attire is expected?
- How are interns evaluated?
- What is the timeline for selecting the intern(s)?

In most cases this information will be disseminated to you during the course of the interview. However, if for some reason some of this information is not covered by the interviewer, you must be prepared to ask questions. Establishing a list of pertinent information that you believe to be important before entering the interview is a good strategy. We suggest that you keep this list of questions in front of you during the interview. As you receive responses to your questions you can check them off your list.

Application

Use this Application to write down the questions you want to ask the interviewer.

Application 6.2: Questions to Ask an Interviewer

List 10 questions that you might ask an interviewer. Arrange your questions from most important (#1) to least important (#10).

Question #1: _____

_____

_____

_____

Question #2: _____

_____

_____

_____

Question #3: _____

_____

_____

_____

Question #4: _____

_____

_____

_____

Question #5: _____

_____

_____

_____

Question #6: _____

_____

_____

_____

Question #7: _____

_____

_____

_____

Question #8: _____

_____

_____

_____

Question #9: _____

_____

_____

_____

Question #10: _____

_____

_____

_____

Practice, Practice, Practice

Interviewing is a skill. Dribbling a basketball, spiking a volleyball, doing a backflip off a diving board or throwing a curve ball all take a great deal of practice—likewise, interviewing skills also need to be practiced. A successful interview depends on many hours of research followed by a great deal of practice. Trying to "wing" an interview will most likely end up in rejection. Do most "first-time" interviewers fail to prepare enough for the interview? In most cases we would give an unequivocal "yes." However, as a result of today's economic conditions and the overwhelming competition for every quality sport-industry position, a first-time interviewee can't afford to be unprepared, unless you plan to move back in with Mom and Dad at 22/23 years of age and go to work at the local mall. That is *not* what you spent the last four years in college preparing for.

Like many skills, answering questions in an interview situation does not come naturally for most of us. The average student finds the interview process to be an anxiety-ridden experience. We have worked diligently doing our research, designing the perfect cover letter, and creating a quality résumé, and during an interview what we say for 30–45 minutes will determine where we may be working for the next few years. Talk about stressful! It takes practice to learn how to relax and answer difficult questions with ease and confidence. It takes practice to learn how to ask important questions of an interviewer without sounding either defensive or aggressive. It also takes practice to eliminate annoying mannerisms or distracting movements during an interview situation.

One of the most effective ways to prepare for an interview is to conduct a "mock" interview. These can be accomplished in a variety of ways. The easiest is to ask a friend or relative to interview you. Establish the type of position you are interested in interviewing for and have your friend or relative ask you a number of questions from Application 6.1. This will give you practice in verbalizing answers that you have already put on paper. Moreover, it will enable you to start practicing your interviewing skills in a very nonthreatening environment. While it may prove valuable to go through the "mock" interview, it is even more important to see yourself. If you don't have the ability to use a video camera, ask someone to use their cell phone. Whatever option you use, it is imperative that you have the chance to view your mannerisms during the interview. Pay particular attention to items such as verbal fillers (i.e., "ums," "uhs," "like," and "you know what I mean"). Also, do you have any annoying mannerisms (i.e., tapping your fingers, stroking your hair, or wringing your hands)? Finally, do you have a difficult time in looking at the interviewer and find yourself looking all around the room?

For a second experience, ask a different individual to develop questions that you haven't seen as yet. This will make you focus on the question being asked; however, due to your previous experience you may feel more comfortable composing responses to the new set of questions. One last type of "mock" experience would be to solicit the assistance of someone already in the sport industry—perhaps an alumnus of your program. We have had success with our athletic director and several alumni conducting these types of interviews once a semester. Our volunteers interview one student while other students sit in the audience as observers. The audience members not only observe the types of questions being asked by practitioners, but they are also able to witness some of the mistakes made by the interviewees.

Finally it is time to go "live." Once you have narrowed down your choices, you need to schedule an interview with a couple of your top selections. Until you gain more experience with interviewing we recommend that you interview in reverse order of importance. For example, if you have three interviews, schedule your third choice as the first interview and keep your first choice for the last interview. That way, a poor interview will not negatively affect where you really want to intern.

Format of Interview

For internships and entry-level positions, the traditional one-on-one, face-to-face style of interview is far and away the most common format. Once you arrive at the agency office, you will normally meet with your immediate supervisor or in some cases a representative from Human Resources. Sometimes that individual is the only one you have any contract with, while at other times you will be shown around the agency and introduced to a variety of individuals. This may take place before or after a formal questioning period; however, important interview questions may also be asked *while* you are being shown around the agency. It is important to remain relaxed and confident. The good news is that you are applying for an internship and not a full-time job.

Unfortunately, some agencies "use" interns in place of hiring full-time employees. In these situations they need interns so desperately that an interview isn't even a consideration. In these situations they try to sell the agency and its benefits to the potential intern. If this ever happens to you, don't forget that you still have a LOT of questions for them. Regardless of whether an interview occurs or not, ensure that you have all of your questions answered while you are there.

Due to the distances involved between the location of the sport agency and the location of the prospective intern's university, a telephone interview may be offered. You must treat this opportunity the same as if it were a traditional face-to-face format and invest the same amount of preparation. Voice quality, inflection, grammar, and word usage are paramount in a telephone interview. We *strongly* urge you to do your interviews in-person, if possible, because you will learn more about a potential agency and supervisor during a face-to-face interview. However, similar to the traditional interview, listen carefully to the questions, ascertain the type of question being asked, and be certain to ask all your questions.

Two main problems occur as a result of a phone interview: 1) telephone interviews do *not* help to prepare you for the job interviews that lie ahead, and 2) telephone interviews do not allow for nonverbal communication. For example, a question posed by the interviewer during a one-on-one interview may be said with a smile. When asked the same question over the phone and not being able to see the smile may leave the interviewee with a completely different impression.

If a formal interview is held, it will usually go through three stages.

1. *Ice breaker.* During this stage of the interview, the interviewer will try to make the interviewee feel comfortable and less anxious. Interviewers have previously sat in the same seat as the interviewee and they know the emotions that the interviewee is experiencing. Frivolous remarks about the weather or who won the big game the night before are two common strategies utilized to put the interviewee at ease. It is during this stage that "open-ended" questions will normally be asked.

2. *Investigation.* This is the "meat" of the interview. The interviewer will attempt to learn all about you. Some open-ended questions may be asked but "probing" questions tend to be the norm. Your previous research pays off in this stage of the interview. If you are prepared this is the stage where you show the interviewer how your experiences meet their needs. This is also the stage where you ask your questions of the interviewer.

3. *Conclusion.* During this stage interviewers will provide a timeline for you as to when you can expect to hear something from them. A variety of "closed-ended" questions may be asked by the interviewer. This is your final chance to ask any questions.

Dress for Success

What is the proper attire for an interview? While the specifics will depend on the job in question, appropriate attire will always demonstrate to the interviewer that you are a professional. This includes any jewelry that is worn. As we have mentioned several times, it is impossible to undo a poor first impression. How you are dressed helps form the first impression for an interviewer. Do you come across as flashy, brazen, conservative, or just plain sloppy? We believe that conservative is always best. Once you are at the agency you can observe how the other employees are clothed. In fact, a very practical question to ask your interviewer would be the dress policy for the business.

As you prepare for the interview look for clothes that are comfortable yet don't look too baggy. Grays, blacks, dark blue, and brown are neutral colors that in most cases are safe to wear. Men, a shirt, tie, and sport coat or suit are the traditional way to dress. Women, a lot depends on your personal preferences. If you are comfortable in a skirt then by all means wear one, though others may want to wear slacks. A business-style suit is perfectly acceptable for women as well. Shoes should be comfortable but basic. Believe it or not, flip flops are not considered to be professional and under no circumstances should they be worn, by either gender. Other accoutrements such as jewelry, perfume/cologne, and hairstyles should also be kept conventional.

These suggestions are obviously dependent on where you plan to interview. If you are interviewing with an action sport, skateboard, or snowboard company then you may get by with a lot more active wear.

Personal freedom of expression is an important issue for many college students. We certainly don't mean to encroach on those beliefs. Be yourself, but remember who makes up the power structure in sport. Right or wrong, good or bad, the majority of power in the business of sport is controlled by older white men. While some of these individuals are adventuresome and free-spirited, the overwhelming majority are conservative. These individuals are the ones who will be deciding your future in the sport industry.

Positive Traits

We previously discussed the importance of confidence during an interview. The interviewer is appraising you from the moment you walk into your interview, so whatever do, do *not* be late! We recommend that you plan to be 10–15 minutes early. Take the extra time to use the restroom. Examine yourself in the mirror. Do your clothes appear smooth and unwrinkled? Is your hair combed properly? Women, if you use make-up, look to ensure it hasn't smeared. While it sounds trivial, check your breath. Bad breath is a guaranteed way to make a poor first impression! We recommend that you bring along a small disposable toothbrush and a small travel-size tube of toothpaste. This ensures fresh-smelling breath and removes anything stuck in your teeth.

From the moment you first meet your interviewer, you need to exude confidence. Simple gestures such as a handshake are important. Be sure to offer a firm grip but remember it is not the time for a milking competition (which too many shakes might suggest). Also, do not make the mistake of shaking a female interviewer's hand less firmly than a male's. Appear relaxed and don't be afraid to greet everyone with a smile. Repeat each person's first name after being introduced; the technique will help you to remember his or her name. Give complete yet concise responses and avoid yes/no responses. You need to demonstrate an interest in the discussion while not trying to take it over. During the interview, it is important to remember that the interviewer is in control. Allow him or her to take the lead. Allow the interviewer to set the tone and pace of an interview. However, remember that you need to assert yourself at the end of the interview if all of your questions/concerns have not been addressed.

You can tell a lot about people by the way they sit. Be sure and sit upright, keep both feet flat on the floor and place your hands in your lap. You don't want to appear robotic, but this isn't the time to start slouching (remember what your mother used to say). Confident people act confidently even while they are not speaking. Acknowledge what others say with a nod, confirming that you are carefully listening to them.

Hearing is a sense; listening is a skill. Concentrate carefully on what is being said. Many people after an interview will admit to feeling exhausted. This is due to several physiological factors, but one of them is the energy it takes to maintain intense concentration. If you do not understand a question, it is perfectly acceptable to ask for clarification. This can actually work to your advantage if you need a moment or two to compose a response. However, if you do not hear a question, an interviewer may have doubts about your listening skills.

We all possess little habits that sometimes reflect our emotions. Tapping a pencil or running your fingers through your hair demonstrates nervousness. It is natural to be nervous during an internship interview. Good interviewers understand this, and they won't judge you harshly if you appear a little nervous or make a mistake during the interview. If this happens, feel free to admit your nervousness, take a second to relax and restore your confidence, then continue with the interview.

Avoid negativity and sarcasm. While your university experience may not have been a positive one, do not make disparaging remarks. Also refrain from negative or sarcastic statements about a previous supervisor. Be positive about the people you have worked for. It is amazing how small the sport industry is and who knows whom. Your interviewer may actually know someone you have worked with in the past.

Following Up After an Interview

Interviews are not completely over once you leave the sport organization. Some people make the mistake of doing nothing after the interview. This is a BIG mistake. It has been estimated that only 36% of job seekers send thank-you notes, yet over 75% of executives think that such notes are an important aspect of the hiring process (*Centre Daily Times,* September 9, 2007, p. D9).

Many individuals in the sport industry recognize the importance of writing a short thank-you note to the agency with whom you interviewed. You notice that we said "note" and not "e-mail." Anyone can send an e-mail; it takes little effort and in many cases is considered to be too casual. Be professional, go "old school," and buy a simple card. Inside the card, write two or three lines expressing your appreciation for the interview. This is a professional way of reconnecting with the organization while reemphasizing your interest in the position. Finally, this note allows you to add any information you may have forgotten to convey during the interview. Be sure to send your thank-you letter as soon as possible after the interview.

Self-Evaluation

Your follow-up should also include a self-evaluation of your interview performance. To conduct your self-evaluation, answer the following questions.

- Was your physical appearance appropriate? Do you feel you gave the impression of a well-groomed, healthy individual?
- Did you speak clearly, distinctly, and refrain from using inappropriate words such as *yeah, nope, and-uh, um, aahhh, like, you know,* or *anyways*?
- Were your answers direct, clear, and concise? Do you feel they were understood by the interviewer(s)?
- Did you use effective nonverbal communication?
- Were you self-confident, open, and at ease in your responses?
- Did you display enthusiasm for the agency and its services?
- What do you feel were your strong points or strengths during the interview?
- What do you feel were your weaknesses and what steps will you take to improve upon them during future interviews?
- How would you rate your overall performance?

SAMPLE THANK-YOU LETTER #1

DATE of Typing

Calvin Funkhouser
Director of Corporate & Suite Sales
Akron Aeros Baseball Club
300 South Main Street
Akron, OH 44308

Dear Mr. Funkhouser:

Thank you for taking the time to interview me for an internship position with the Akron Aeros Baseball Club. I was extremely impressed with both the team staff as well as with the stadium itself.

As you know, my career goal is to become an inside sales representative for a Major League Baseball team. My visit with the Aeros has reaffirmed this goal, and I am excited about the possibility of doing an internship under your supervision.

During the interview, you requested that I send you a sample of my writing. Enclosed is a copy of a paper I wrote entitled "Marketing a Minor League Baseball Club: Are Popcorn, Peanuts, and Cracker Jacks Enough?" This paper was written last semester for SPMT 394 (Sport Marketing).

Thank you again for the interview, and I look forward to hearing from you soon.

Sincerely,

Christina Clementi
1248 South Franklin Avenue
Somerset, PA 15501
814-441-2531

Enclosure

SAMPLE THANK-YOU LETTER #2

44 Rocky Top Road
Cold Springs, PA 18432
843-230-3872

DATE of Typing

Ms. Adeline Watts
Guest Services / Tour Manager
PSSI Stadium Corporation
30 Rooney Ave.
Pittsburgh, PA 15210

Dear Ms. Watts:

I enjoyed meeting you last Thursday and appreciate your interviewing me for an internship position with PSSI Stadium Corporation. I especially want to thank you for providing me with an extensive tour of Heinz Field.

During the interview, you expressed interest in knowing more about my practicum experience working at Beaver Stadium in State College, PA. Enclosed is an evaluation completed by my practicum supervisor, Paul Bardenschwartz. I spoke with Mr. Bardenschwartz, and he stated he would be happy to speak with you about my experience. He can be reached at 814-801-9190.

Once again, thank you for the interview and tour. I look forward to hearing from you as soon as a decision is made regarding the internship position.

Sincerely,

Anthony Smith

Enclosure

Handling Rejection

As Dolly Parton was fond of saying, "if you want the rainbow, you gotta put up with a little rain." No matter how good we think we are, we sometimes fail. A good résumé and creative cover letter may not be enough. Perhaps you didn't have the experience they were looking for, you may not have been as qualified as another candidate, or perhaps you had a poor interview. Regardless of why you weren't selected, you can always learn from every rejection. First of all, do not take it personally. In most situations sport agencies are looking for specific skill sets and yours may not have been a good fit. A sport analogy would be a quarterback who was unsuccessful with one team because of their offensive philosophy. He moves to a team with a different offensive philosophy, and suddenly he is very successful. Did his skill set suddenly become better? No, it didn't match the first team but meshed perfectly with the second team.

Turn every rejection into a learning experience. Look at your résumé. Is it reflective of who you are? Did it match the position? Was your cover letter creative and unflawed? Replay the interview in your mind. Was there anything you could have done differently? Were you extremely nervous? Were you unable to answer a question? We suggest that a week or so after not being selected call the interviewer and ask for his assessment. Explain that you want to learn from your interview and did he or she have any suggestions on how you could be better prepared for the next interview. Following up with an interviewer after rejection will demonstrate your interest in improving your interview skills, and it will keep your name in the interviewer's mind should another internship opening occur.

Student Perspective

Here are some additional comments from various sport management alums on what they considered to be important pertaining to the interview process.

Before a phone interview, research the organization extensively on the Internet, and come up with questions of your own, such as:

- What kind of hands-on experience will I gain?
- How do you think this internship will prepare me for a career in sport?
- What are your expectations?
- How do you describe yourself as a supervisor?
- Will you be able to assist me in finding a place to live?
- How will I be able to take care of utilities and other household needs?

Follow your heart and dream big. Think outside of your 'comfort zone' and try to get an internship in an area that you really want to work in, rather than an internship that just fulfills part of your coursework If you pick an internship that you are interested in—that you would love and enjoy—your time there will be very beneficial to you. It will seem like you really aren't doing work but rather starting your career. Don't be afraid to ask questions on your interview. The last thing you want to do is not ask questions and then get stuck working an internship that it totally different from what you have expected or wanted. Stay true to yourself and everything else will fall into place. A point I'd like to stress about the interview process is not to limit yourself to a certain geographical area, as I did. Tell the interviewer that you will move anywhere. With sport it may take a drastic change in surroundings to realize that dream job. Now that I have graduated, I have finally opened myself up to the idea of moving away to a job I would love.

Sales is a must. In today's sport industry, directors and general managers could care less if you are the best PowerPoint slide maker in the world, or if you are the top of your class in this or that. If you cannot sell a ticket or sponsorship, you will not get very far in today's business. Whether you are involved with grounds keeping, stadium operations, or mascot relations, at some point you will need to be able to sell. During your interview, mention this ability and interest. It could be the difference between being chosen and driving home in despair.

Thanks to Bill Blood, Jakub Jaroswiecz, Megan Powell, and Brian Thompson.

Summary

This chapter has covered a lot of information pertaining to the interview. Proper preparation will be your number-one ally during the interview process. Remember that your previous experiences have shaped you into a valuable sport manager. Therefore, you have a lot to offer a potential internship site, and the interview should be a two-way exchange. You want to convey to the interviewer the positive assets that you can bring to the organization and how they connect to agencies' needs. We have provided you with a variety of strategies that will assist you as you begin interviewing. Following these concepts will give you added confidence.

Chapter Seven
Selection and Final Planning

In any moment of decision the best thing you can do is the right thing, the next best thing is the wrong thing, and the worst thing you can do is nothing.

---Theodore Roosevelt---

You have now created your game plan for success, you have designed a professional-looking cover letter, and you have put together a quality résumé. You used all those tools to identify multiple internship locations. You narrowed the locations down to two or three high-quality opportunities and you have completed the interview process. Whew! The hard part is over… not so fast, my fine friend. Now the hard part actually *begins:* which of the internship locations do you select? If you haven't been fortunate enough to receive multiple offers your choice is quite simple, but you still need to consider if the one offer will meet your academic, personal, and professional needs.

Making Your Selection

The internship you select will, if you have completed all the previous stages correctly, put you one step closer to your desired career in the sport industry. Therefore, this decision needs to be made with a great deal of thought and careful consideration. As with all major decisions it is good to solicit the advice of those whose opinions you value and respect. Your parents, family, friends and academic professors may provide valuable advice, but ultimately the decision must be yours and yours alone. Wanting to live near your parents, close to your significant other or your friends are all admirable reasons, but making a decision of where to complete your internship based entirely on your proximity to others could be a disastrous decision. Decide what is *best* for you and your future career. The internship that meets *that* criterion may be many miles or states away.

The applications we have provided for you to complete plus the information gleaned from your interview, in most cases, have given you valuable information to make your final decision. However, if you are indecisive, consider the following questions.

If I did my internship at *(name of the agency),* would I be able to:

1. Refine and acquire professional skills important to my career? (see Application 1.3)
2. Do the type of work I enjoy most? (see Application 2.1)
3. Provide the experience in the kind of professional position I ultimately want to have? (see Application 2.1 and Application 2.3)
4. Meet my internship goals? (see Application 2.2)
5. Meet my most important internship needs and preferences? (see Application 3.3)
6. Feel comfortable working with the people I met during my interview?

Application

The previous questions may have helped to solidify one internship location over another. Even if you only had one offer it would be a good idea to answer the questions pertaining to your one option. If the responses don't meet with your approval you may need to rethink your internship opportunity.

The last thing in the world you want to do is to "settle" for an internship. "Settling" means you have no other offers and instead of accepting an internship that will help you to successfully fulfill your game plan, you take anything that is offered. In most instances we term these as *dead-end internships*. An example of a dead-end internship is one that uses interns in place of full-time employees. Or they may be an agency that hasn't hired any previous intern for years. Some agencies that provide these types of internships will often offer you a position without even conducting an interview. We have heard of some agencies who will offer a student an internship over the telephone… without even seeing his or her résumé! These types of agencies should be avoided at *all* costs. How effective would an intern be in successfully fulfilling his or her game plan after completing such an experience?

If, after answering the previous questions, one agency doesn't stand out over the others you may need to complete the Internship Agency Evaluation Form (Application 7.1). After listing the pros and cons of each agency, your decision will be easier to make.

Application 7.1: Internship Agency Evaluation Form

Take some time to identify the pros and cons of doing an internship with the following agency. Then, compare this list with the pros and cons offered by other agencies you are considering. This comparison will help you decide which agency offers you the best internship.

Name of Agency _____

PROS	CONS
1. _____	1. _____
2. _____	2. _____
3. _____	3. _____
4. _____	4. _____
5. _____	5. _____
6. _____	6. _____
7. _____	7. _____
8. _____	8. _____
9. _____	9. _____
10. _____	10. _____
11. _____	11. _____
12. _____	12. _____
13. _____	13. _____
14. _____	14. _____
15. _____	15. _____
16. _____	16. _____
17. _____	17. _____
18. _____	18. _____
19. _____	19. _____
20. _____	20. _____

Final Comments from the Students

Here are some final comments from various sport management alumni on what they considered to be important pertaining to the selection process:

It was just a gut feeling and a right fit for me. I wasn't offered more than one, but as soon as I started pursuing my internship I immediately stopped pursuing the other one I was interested in. I knew this was the one I wanted.

Once I accepted the internship, I continued to research the company so I knew as much going in as I could. Even though I acquired some business clothing during my senior year, I still did not have enough to wear on a daily basis. Therefore, I invested in some more work clothes. Dress for success.

I selected my internship with the Houston Astros over the Detroit Ignition of the Indoor Soccer League because I felt the Astros gave me a much better opportunity to grow as a sport professional than the Ignition. The Ignition wanted me to do an operation internship and help them with the setup and take-down of the field for events. They also wanted me to help out with ticket sales and promotions. I felt the Astros gave me a better chance to succeed. It was the best decision I have made.

During my senior year at SRU, I had what I considered to be two major internship offers. My first was with FOX Sports in LA and my other was to intern with the United States Olympic Committee in Colorado Springs. I really struggled with which one to take—both were wonderful opportunities— both would offer me a fantastic networking system as well as give me the ability to really utilize what I learned in my classes. However, at the end of the day it all came down to finances. The USOC was offering housing, meals, and a small stipend. Fox Sports was not—I was responsible for 100% of my living expenses. If I had to do it all again, I would make the exact same decision. The knowledge I gained, the networks I made, the friendships I made proved to me it really was a once in a lifetime opportunity. To this day I am still asked about it on job interviews.

I selected my internship based on several options. I wanted to travel and see new things so I knew staying in Pennsylvania was not a good option. The two offers I had were in Florida and California. California was the better opportunity because it was working in baseball, compared to Florida which was more of hospitality and event management opportunity.

Thanks to Jason Hannold, Jakub Jaroswiecz, Dana Maalouf, Megan Powell, and A. J. Turkovich.

Notification

As Walt Disney used to say, "If you can dream it, you can do it." You are *very* close to realizing your dream, but you still need to finalize the process. Once you have determined which internship offer to accept, you need to notify the agency. Regardless if you do this by phone (often the most expeditious method) or not, you still need to write an acceptance letter. It provides the agency with something in writing that documents your intention, besides which it is the professional thing to do. During the notification process you should confirm important information at this time, such as pay or stipend, work responsibilities, starting date, and length of internship. We have provided two examples of acceptance letters for your examination.

Once you have confirmed your first choice, you need to notify the other sport businesses that you have decided to go in a different direction. Again, not only is this considered a professional courtesy, but it allows the declined agency the opportunity to contact their second choice in a timely fashion. Imagine the appreciation of the student who happens to be the declined agency's second choice. This student may be anxiously waiting to hear from the agency you are declining, and if you do not decline the offer in a timely fashion, he or she may be forced to accept a less desirable internship.

Oftentimes sending the declined agency a letter will prove difficult, but your professionalism will be recognized by that sport business and might help you at some point in the future. In the letter, thank them for their consideration and be sure to explain the reasons for your decision. Two sample letters declining an internship are included for your perusal.

SAMPLE ACCEPTANCE LETTER #1

DATE of Typing

Karen Fitzpatrick
Associate Athletic Director
Thiel College
75 College Avenue
Greenville, PA 16125

Dear Ms. Fitzpatrick:

I am pleased to accept your offer of an internship in the sports information department at Thiel College. After visiting the college in December, I knew that your program was ideally suited to my professional interests, and I am very excited about the learning opportunities available to me.

As I mentioned during our phone conversation, my internship is scheduled to begin on May 10th and end on July 30th. It is my understanding that I will work 40 hours per week, receive a $150 weekly stipend, and be supervised by you. I enjoyed meeting you during my visit, and look forward to what you can teach me about media relations as well as the expansion of services and features available to fans and the media via the Internet.

Thank you for offering me an internship with Thiel, and I look forward to seeing you in May.

Sincerely,

Ben Mitchell
145 East Church Street
Homer City, PA 15748
724-555-9834

SAMPLE ACCEPTANCE LETTER #2

DATE of Typing

Kari Samora
Disney's Wide World of Sports
710 Victory Way
Kissimmee, FL 34747

Dear Ms. Samora:

Thank you for offering me an internship position with Disney's Wide World of Sports. As I indicated during my interview, working for Disney will provide the type of learning environment I am seeking; therefore, I enthusiastically accept your offer.

I hope to begin my 12-week internship on June 7, but I will call you within the next two weeks to confirm dates and make other necessary arrangements. You will also soon receive documents from Dr. Robin Ammon, my internship supervisor at Slippery Rock University. He will confirm my placement and provide you with additional information about Slippery Rock's internship program.

Thanks again for offering me an internship position. I am looking forward to learning from you and your excellent staff.

Sincerely,

Brian A. Thompson
171 Moraine Drive
Portersville, PA 16057
412-555-2602

SAMPLE LETTER OF DECLINE #1

18 Eaglecrest Dr.
Lakewood, CO 80226
303-555-4707

DATE of Typing

Ms. Nikkie Reid
Manager
Better Bodies Fitness Center
7777 West Jewell Ave.
Lakewood, CO 80232

Dear Ms. Reid:

Thank you for your offer of an internship at Better Bodies Fitness Center. As you know, I was very impressed with your operation, and enjoyed meeting you and your excellent staff.

I am certain that an internship under your supervision would be a valuable learning experience for any student. However, I must decline your generous offer. After careful consideration, I have decided to do my internship at Fitness Plus at Pinehurst Country Club in Littleton. As you know, I am also interested in event planning and Fitness Plus offers me the opportunity to combine fitness management along with planning golf tournaments.

Thank you for your consideration and for the courtesy that you and your staff extended to me. Perhaps we will have the opportunity to work together in the future.

Sincerely,

Mary Fitzgerald

SAMPLE LETTER OF DECLINE #2

DATE of Typing

Calvin Funkhouser
Director of Corporate & Suite Sales
Akron Aeros Baseball Club
300 South Main Street
Akron, OH 44308

Dear Mr. Funkhouser:

I would like to thank you again for my interview on February 16th, and I sincerely appreciate your willingness to supervise my senior internship. As much as I appreciate your offer, however, I am afraid I must decline at this time.

Although the Akron Aeros are an exceptional minor league baseball team, the limitation of only being able to work on game-days would make it very difficult for me to achieve my internship goals in a timely fashion. I have, therefore, decided to accept a full-time internship with the Reading Phillies.

Thanks again for offering me an internship position, and please extend my appreciation to your staff for their hospitality during my interview. I thoroughly enjoyed meeting all of you.

Sincerely,

Christina Clementi
1248 South Franklin Avenue
Somerset, PA 15501
814-555-2501

Almost all of the preliminary work is completed. However, as with any other major decision, a great deal of preparation needs to take place before the internship actually commences. This is especially true if you select a sport agency far from home. The following information will help you plan for your internship experience.

Communication

Research has demonstrated that communication is the single most important element in a successful internship experience. Therefore it is vital that you establish proper channels of communication with your internship supervisor. At the same time, you need to ensure that proper lines of communication exist between you and whoever is your university internship supervisor. In many instances you are quite familiar with this individual, which helps to negate any problems. However, in some cases your university internship supervisor may be someone who you don't know very well. In this situation the importance of an open line of communication cannot be overstated.

Professionalism

Most of your sport management programs have emphasized professionalism since you were a freshman (i.e., proper attire for business situations, respect for those in the industry, proper grammar, and ability to work with others). For many of you, however, the internship is the first chance you will have to actually practice being a professional in the "real world."

Intern Apparel

Some agencies provide uniforms for employees and interns to wear. Other than those situations, you will be held responsible for dressing the part. The easiest way to meet expectations is to *ask* and not *assume*. In most cases, for either gender a nice pair of slacks and a collared shirt will suffice. Females could also wear a skirt and blouse. However, some sport agencies expect more formal business attire. Some sport businesses will require you to dress up for most of the week and then have one "casual day." As we mentioned, asking your supervisor will help alleviate any type of misunderstanding or embarrassing situations.

Expenses

Selecting the best internship often requires a certain degree of risk. It may require you to travel and live in a completely different part of the country and, in some unique situations, in a different country. Making a choice to complete such an internship in many cases will lead to new experiences and hopefully a great entry-level position into a sport business, but a certain investment goes along with the decision. Moving costs, lodging, and other accompanying expenditures must be planned for very carefully. In some cases the sport agency may be able to provide housing for interns or sometimes housing at a reduced cost. Others expect the intern to pay for everything. If the sport agency has games or entertainment events, sometimes the intern may be paid to work the events. Ask your internship supervisor if they have any suggestions for ways you could earn additional income.

Resources and References

Depending on the location of your internship, various resources may be utilized. Many sites (such as professional sports teams) will provide all the necessary resources for you to carry out your duties and responsibilities. For other smaller agencies your textbooks, course projects, and class notes may prove beneficial. Without a doubt, having a personal laptop computer will be a definite benefit regardless of the size of the sport agency.

Orientation

An orientation is a training session provided for new employees. Due to the litigious nature of our society and to ensure productivity, most sport businesses now include interns in their new employee orientations. Most sport agencies have excellent orientation programs, but you still need to do your homework before starting your internship. Any information that is provided to you prior to your first day on the internship should be scrutinized before reporting for work. This information may contain important details such as where to park, proper attire, miscellaneous rules and regulations, as well as other relevant facts.

At the same time you should have developed your own set of questions to ask during the orientation. Most of your questions will undoubtedly be answered during the orientation but, just in case, be prepared to pose your own questions. Some of your concerns may be similar to the following questions. Feel free to add any of them to your list.

- To whom do I report? If my immediate supervisor is not available, then to whom do I report?
- What is appropriate attire on the job? Are there any aspects of the internship that require other types of attire?
- What are the agency's emergency medical procedures (EMPs)?
- Do I need keys to any of the areas in the facility? If so, who issues them?
- If your university doesn't require you to carry your own liability insurance (and we *highly* encourage you to have a liability insurance policy), does the sport agency provide liability insurance for interns?
- What are the procedures if an employee, guest, or client is injured or needs medical attention?
- Are personal leave days allowed for interns? If so, what are the procedures for requesting a personal leave day?
- If I am sick and unable to work, to whom do I report my illness?
- Are interns notified if the agency will not be open due to severe weather? If not, how can I find out if the agency will be closed?
- Is there a company directory that is available for interns?
- Are there any policies, procedures, or restrictions that apply to interns on the job?
- What are the procedures for evaluation of interns? Are there specific forms that are used? If so, would they provide you with a blank form to help guide your behavior during the internship?

Summary

We designed this final chapter to assist in your decision about which internship to select. Therefore, it is the culmination of your game plan for success. The selection of your internship site will be one of the most important decisions you ever make as it should be the first step in the progression of events that incorporates your game plan. However, once you have made the selection your work is not yet completed. As a burgeoning sport management professional, you must realize the importance of communication. A thank-you letter or letter declining the internship is the final step. This courtesy will help to cement your personal network of sport industry contacts.

Final Comment from Authors

Congratulations on completing this manual. We hope you have been able to incorporate some of our strategies and tips in securing a quality internship. We created this manual to assist sport management students in securing their first internship. However, the strategies would be the same if you needed a second internship or if you sought full-time employment. The important idea is to utilize this manual as well as its applications as you begin your journey towards a career in sport management. This manual is only as strong as the information contained in it. If you have any comments or suggestions, we would certainly appreciate hearing from you. Feel free to send us examples of cover letters or résumés that we can include in the next edition! Contact information is on the following page.

Author Information

Robin Ammon Jr., EdD
135 Winterwood Dr
Butler, PA 16001

Matthew Walker, PhD
Sport Management Program
University of Florida
242B Florida Gym
PO Box 118208
Gainesville, FL 32611-8208

Appendices
Online Resources

This section provides a list of websites that may help you in your internship search process. Although not listed here, many sport entities have their own websites with employment information. We suggest checking with regional organizations to see if they maintain a website or have print materials containing internship or job information. You should also check to see if internship-related online or print materials are available from your internship coordinator, other faculty members, or your university's library.

The following online resources are divided into two sections. The first section provides websites that focus upon sport-related jobs and internships. The second section lists some of the many general career and employment sites available on the Internet. Both sections may help you identify internship and employment opportunities, as well as assist in your job search after graduation. All websites in this appendix were active at the time of publication; however, please keep in mind that websites are sometimes removed from the Internet or they may not be accessible because they have changed their location (URL).

Sport-Related Employment and Internship Sites

Title: AAHPERD Careers
Address: http://www.aahperd.org/careers
Comments: Offers job postings in sport and physical education via CareerLink.

Title: Executive Sports Placement
Address: http://www.prosportsjobs.com/
Comments: Fee-paying service.

Title: InternAbroad.com
Address: http://www.internabroad.com/search.cfm
Comments: Offers comprehensive information for international study and travel. International internship database; search capacity by type of internship, including recreation-related categories; scholarship information; reference materials.

Title: InternSearch.com
Address: http://www.internsearch.com/directory_recres.htm
Comments: Provides information internships available in resort, recreation, and sport management.

Title: JobsInSports.com
Address: http://www.jobsinsports.com/
Comments: Fee-paying service.

Title: National Intramural–Recreational Sports Association's Bluefishjobs.com
Address: http://www.bluefishjobs.com
Comments: Provides information on jobs in intramural sports and recreation-related agencies. Database of vacancies nationally; personal accounts and résumé services; jobseeker help.

Title: NCAA Scholarships and Internships
Address: http://www.ncaa.org
Comments: Internship program through the National Collegiate Athletic Association.

Title: PGA TOUR Diversity Internship
Address: http://www.pgatour.com/company/internships.html
Comments: Well-established, paid 10–12 internship program with the PGA TOUR.
Title: QuintCareers.com
Address: http://www.quintcareers.com/sports_jobs.html
Comments: Provides opportunities in the sport industry while also providing job-hunting tools and career tools.

Title: Sports Agent Blog
Address: http://www.sportsagentblog.com/internships/
Comments: Provides opportunities in the sport law industry.

Title: Sports Careers
Address: http://www.sportscareers.com/
Comments: Provides job opportunities in career development information in the sport industry.

Title: Sport Industry Job Board
Address: http://www.sportsjobboard.com
Comments: Fee-paying service; provides information on employment opportunities in the sport industry for members.

Title: Sports Links Central
Address: http://www.sportslinkscentral.com/sports_business/sports_jobs.htm
Comments: Provides a comprehensive listing of links to sport internship websites.

Title: Teamwork Online
Address: http://www.teamworkonline.com/
Comments: Provides opportunities in college sports, professional leagues, and other sport franchises. Includes an applicant tracking system, into which you can upload the résumé.

Title: United States Golf Association PJ Boatwright Internship Program
Address: http://www.usga.org/jobs/internships/golf_administration/Internships/
Comments: Provides opportunities with state and regional golf associations in golf event management, tournament operations, membership services, and junior golf programs.

Title: Women's Sports Foundation
Address: http://www.womensportsfoundation.org
Comments: Internships available working directly with the Foundation.

Title: Women's Sports Jobs
Address: http://www.womenssportsjobs.com
Comments: Career information for women's sports jobs, career counseling, and résumé writing services.

Title: WorkinSports.com
Address: http://www.workinsports.com/
Comments: Comprehensive site listing league and team opportunities. The site does require a paid membership.

General Career, Employment, and Internship Sites

Title: AfterCollege.com
Address: http://www.jobresource.com
Comments: Features employment and internship database, plus other career information. Free registration; résumé services; advice and assistance; alumni network.

Title: America's Job Bank
Address: http://www.ajb.org
Comments: Includes comprehensive job-related services and information. Database with over one million jobs nationally; online résumé service; automated job search.

Title: Athletic Business
Address: http://www.athleticbusiness.com
Comments: Includes comprehensive articles, buyers' guides, and current news regarding athletics, fitness, and recreation. Monthly magazine and online article search available.

Title: Black Collegian Online
Address: http://www.blackcollegian.com
Comments: Provides extensive job-related services and information for African-American job seekers. Database with search options; employer profiles; feature articles; online résumé service.

Title: CareerJournal
Address: http://online.wsj.com/careers
Comments: *Wall Street Journal* site provides the day's top job-related stories and includes "Job Hunting Tips" and "Find a Job" features. Also provides links to an extensive list of high-quality editorial content, databases, and other employment-related services.

Title: Careermag.com
Address: http://www.careermag.com
Comments: Offers extensive job-related services and information. Automated search capacity; online résumé service; reference materials and articles.

Title: CareerSite.com
Address: http://400.careersite.com/?pid=104
Comments: Provides comprehensive database of jobs listed in newspapers nationally. Keyword search capacity; online résumé service; company profiles; news and resources.

Title: CollegeGrad.com
Address: http://www.collegegrad.com
Comments: Includes internship and employment database, plus employment services and information. Career planning and job-seeking information; résumé services; job-related forum.

Title: College News
Address: http://www.collegenews.com
Comments: Lists internships and employment opportunities, as well as extensive employment services and information. Listings by category; career planning information.

Title: Columbus Internships
Address: http://www.columbusinternships.com
Comments: Lists internships across the Columbus, Ohio region. Requires users to sign up; cover letter and résumé resources.

Title: HotJobs.Yahoo.com
Address: http://www.hotjobs.yahoo.com
Comments: Provides a number of job-related features, including employment listings, job-search articles, and career-related questions and answers.

Title: Internet Career Connection
Address: http://www.iccweb.com
Comments: Provides comprehensive career services and information. National and international database of jobs and internships; keyword, category, or location search capacity; advice on searching for jobs, including government or state positions.

Title: Internet Job Source
Address: http://www.statejobs.com
Comments: Lists jobs by state, including government and private openings. Keyword search capacity; job-related links.

Title: InternJobs.com
Address: http://internjobs.com
Comments: Provides comprehensive internship information. Database of internships nationally; keyword or location search capacity; links to the AboutJobs.com network.

Title: InternshipPrograms.com
Address: http://www.internshipprograms.com/
Comments: An internship search engine. Allows students to post résumés and search an internship database, with some opportunities in recreation-related organizations. Registration required.

Title: Job Source Network
Address: http://www.jobsourcenetwork.com
Comments: Provides links to comprehensive career services and information.

Title: Job-Hunt.org
Address: http://www.job-hunt.org
Comments: Offers comprehensive career-related services and information. Database of job listings; online résumé service; career tools; reference materials and articles; links to other career sites.

Title: Job-Interview.net
Address: http://www.job-interview.net
Comments: Offers an extensive collection of interview-related information, including interview questions, tips for interviewees, and suggestions to prepare for an interview.

Title: JobWeb.com
Address: http://www.jobweb.com
Comments: Excellent collection of articles and advice for students seeking jobs and internships. Features include marketing yourself, résumé and interview advice and a free subscription to a monthly career-related publication for students and graduates.

Title: Monster.com
Address: http://www.monster.com
Comments: Provides extensive job-related services and information. Over one million national and international job listings; online résumé service; automated job search; reference materials.

Title: Quintessential Careers
Address: http://www.quintcareers.com
Comments: Offers comprehensive job-related services and information. Reference materials and articles; career tool kit; searchable database; fee-based résumé service; free online newsletter.

Title: USInterns.com
Address: http://www.usinterns.com
Comments: Provides links to searchable database with thousands of internship opportunities.

Title: WinWay
Address: http://www.winway.com
Comments: Provides résumé and job-search information. Extensive links to job-related sites.

Title: Yahoo! Careers
Address: http://careers.yahoo.com
Comments: Offers many employment-related services and features. Database of job listings; online résumé service; keyword job search; career tools; reference materials and articles.

Additional Sites

American Alliance of Health, Physical Education, Recreation, and Dance (AAHPERD)
1900 Association Drive
Reston, VA 22091
(800) 213-7193
http://www.aahperd.org

Club Managers Association of America
1733 King Street
Alexandria, VA 22314
(703) 739-9500
http://www.nccgolf.org

International Health, Racquet, and Sportsclub Association
263 Summer Street
Boston, MA 02210
(800) 228-4772 or (617) 951-0055
http://www.ihrsa.org

North American Society for Sport Management
NASSM Business Office
West Gym 117
Slippery Rock University
Slippery Rock, PA 16057
(724) 738-4812
http://www.nassm.com

International Association of Assembly Managers
635 Fritz Dr., Suite 100
Coppell, TX 75019-4442
(972) 906-7441
http://www.iaam.org/

Recommended Readings

Bennett, S. (2005). *The elements of résumé style*. New York: AMACOM.

Beshara, T. (2005). *The job search solution: The ultimate system for finding a great job now!* New York: AMACOM.

Betrus, M. (2005). *Perfect phrases for cover letters*. New York: McGraw-Hill.

Block, J., & Betrus, M. (2004). *Great answers! Great questions! For your job interview*. New York: McGraw-Hill.

Bolles, R. N. (2007). *What color is your parachute?: A practical manual for job-hunters and career-changers*. Berkeley, CA: Ten Speed Press.

Bright, J., & Earl, J. (2006). *Amazing résumés: What employers want to see—and how to say it*. Indianapolis, IN: JIST Works.

Carter, C. (2004). *Majoring in the rest of your life: Career secrets for college students* (4th ed.). New York: The Noonday Press.

Dickel, M. R., & Roehm, F. E. (2008). *The guide to Internet job searching*. New York: McGraw-Hill.

Enelow, W., & Boldt, A. (2006). *No-nonsense cover letters: The essential guide to creating attention-grabbing cover letters that get interviews & job offers*. Franklin Lakes, NJ: Career Press.

Epstein, L. (2007). *You're hired! Interview skills to get the job*. Arlington, VA: E3 Publishing.

Farr, J. M. (2007). *Getting the job you really want: A step-by-step guide to finding a good job in less time* (5th ed.). Indianapolis, IN: JIST Publishing.

Fox, J. (2007). *How to land your dream job: No résumé! And other secrets to get you in the door*. New York: Hyperion.

Greene, B. (2004). *Get the interview every time: Fortune 500 hiring professionals' tips for writing winning résumés and cover letters*. Chicago: Dearborn Trade Publishing.

Hachey, J. (2007). *The big guide to living and working overseas: 3,045 career building resources* (4th ed. revised). Toronto, ON, Canada: Intercultural Systems.

Kador, J. (2002). *201 best questions to ask on your interview*. New York: McGraw-Hill.

Kennedy, J. L. (2007). *Résumés for dummies* (5th ed). Hoboken, NJ: Wiley.

Kessler, R. (2006). *Competency-based interviews: Master the tough new interview style and give them the answers that will win you the job*. Franklin Lakes, NJ: Career Press.

Kessler, R., & Strasburg, L. A. (2005). *Competency-based résumé: How to bring your résumé to the top of the pile*. Franklin Lakes, NJ: Career Press.

Krannich, R. L., & Krannich, C. R. (2007). *No one will hire me! Avoid 17 mistakes and win the job* (3rd ed.). Manassas Park, VA: Impact.

Landes, M. (2005). *The back door guide to short-term adventures: Internships, extraordinary experiences, seasonal jobs, volunteering, work abroad* (4th ed.). Berkeley, CA: Ten Speed Press.

Levinson, J., & Perry, D. (2005). *Guerrilla marketing for job hunters: 400 unconventional tips, tricks, and tactics for landing your dream job*. Hoboken, NJ: John Wiley & Sons.

Medley, H. A. (2005). *Sweaty palms: The neglected art of being interviewed*. New York: Time Warner.

Nobel, D. F. (2007). *Gallery of best résumés: A collection of quality résumés by professional résumé writers* (4th ed.). Indianapolis, IN: JIST Publishing.

Oliver, V. (2005). *301 Smart answers to tough interview questions*. Naperville, IL: Sourcebooks.

Rosenberg, A. D., & Hizer, D. V. (2007). *The résumé handbook: How to write outstanding résumés and cover letters for every situation* (5th ed.). Boston: Adams Media.

Ryan, D. J. (2004). *Job search handbook for people with disabilities* (2nd ed.). Indianapolis, IN: JIST Publishing.

Satterthwaite, F., & D'Orsi, G. (2003). *The career portfolio workbook*. New York: McGraw-Hill.

Taylor, J., & Hardy, D. (2005). *Monster careers: Interviewing: Master the moment that gets you the job*. New York: Penguin Group.

Van Devender, J., & Van Devender-Graves, G. (2007). *Savvy interviewing: How to ace the interview & get the job*. Herndon, VA: Capital Books.

Wallace, R. (2006). *Adams cover letter almanac*. Avon, MA: Adams Media.

Walsh, R. (2007). *The complete job search book for college students: A step-by-step guide to finding the right job* (3rd ed.). Avon, MA: Adams Media.

Whitcomb, S. (2006). *Résumé magic: Trade secrets of a professional résumé writer*. Indianapolis, IN: JIST Works.

Yates, M. J. (2006). *Cover letters that knock 'em dead*. Avon, MA: Adams Media.

Yates, M. J. (2006). *Résumés that knock 'em dead* (7th ed.). Avon, MA: Adams Media.

Other Books by Venture Publishing, Inc.

File o' Fun: A Recreation Planner for Games & Activities, Third Edition
    by Jane Harris Ericson and Diane Ruth Albright
The Game and Play Leader's Handbook: Facilitating Fun and Positive Interaction, Revised Edition
    by Bill Michaelis and John M. O'Connell
The Game Finder—A Leader's Guide to Great Activities
    by Annette C. Moore
Getting People Involved in Life and Activities: Effective Motivating Techniques
    by Jeanne Adams
Hands On! Children's Activities for Fairs, Festivals, and Special Events
    by Karen L. Ramey
Health Promotion for Mind, Body, and Spirit
    by Suzanne Fitzsimmons and Linda L. Buettner
In Search of the Starfish: Creating a Caring Environment
    by Mary Hart, Karen Primm, and Kathy Cranisky
Inclusion: Including People With Disabilities in Parks and Recreation Opportunities
    by Lynn Anderson and Carla Brown Kress
Inclusive Leisure Services: Responding to the Rights of People with Disabilities, Second Edition
    by John Dattilo
Internships in Recreation and Leisure Services: A Practical Guide for Students, Fourth Edition
    by Edward E. Seagle, Jr. and Ralph W. Smith
Interpretation of Cultural and Natural Resources, Second Edition
    by Douglas M. Knudson, Ted T. Cable, and Larry Beck
Intervention Activities for At-Risk Youth
    by Norma J. Stumbo
Introduction to Outdoor Recreation: Providing and Managing Resource Based Opportunities
    by Roger L. Moore and B.L. Driver
Introduction to Recreation and Leisure Services, Eighth Edition
    by Karla A. Henderson, M. Deborah Bialeschki, John L. Hemingway, Jan S. Hodges, Beth D. Kivel, and H. Douglas Sessoms
Introduction to Therapeutic Recreation: U.S. and Canadian Perspectives
    by Kenneth Mobily and Lisa Ostiguy
Introduction to Writing Goals and Objectives: A Manual for Recreation Therapy Students and Entry-Level Professionals
    by Suzanne Melcher
Leadership and Administration of Outdoor Pursuits, Third Edition
    by James Blanchard, Michael Strong, and Phyllis Ford
Leadership in Leisure Services: Making a Difference, Third Edition
    by Debra J. Jordan
Leisure and Leisure Services in the 21st Century: Toward Mid Century
    by Geoffrey Godbey
The Leisure Diagnostic Battery Computer Software (CD)
    by Peter A. Witt, Gary Ellis, and Mark A. Widmer
Leisure Education I: A Manual of Activities and Resources, Second Edition
    by Norma J. Stumbo
Leisure Education II: More Activities and Resources, Second Edition
    by Norma J. Stumbo
Leisure Education III: More Goal-Oriented Activities
    by Norma J. Stumbo

Leisure Education IV: Activities for Individuals with Substance Addictions
by Norma J. Stumbo
Leisure Education Program Planning: A Systematic Approach, Third Edition
by John Dattilo
Leisure for Canadians
edited by Ron McCarville and Kelly MacKay
Leisure Studies: Prospects for the Twenty-First Century
edited by Edgar L. Jackson and Thomas L. Burton
Leisure in Your Life: New Perspectives
by Geoffrey Godbey
Making a Difference in Academic Life: A Handbook for Park, Recreation, and Tourism Educators and Graduate Students
edited by Dan Dustin and Tom Goodale
Managing to Optimize the Beneficial Outcomes of Leisure
edited by B. L. Driver
Marketing in Leisure and Tourism: Reaching New Heights
by Patricia Click Janes
The Melody Lingers On: A Complete Music Activities Program for Older Adults
by Bill Messenger
More Than a Game: A New Focus on Senior Activity Services
by Brenda Corbett
The Multiple Values of Wilderness
by H. Ken Cordell, John C. Bergstrom, and J.M. Bowker
N.E.S.T. Approach: Dementia Practice Guidelines for Disturbing Behaviors
by Linda L. Buettner and Suzanne Fitzsimmons
The Organizational Basis of Leisure Participation: A Motivational Exploration
by Robert A. Stebbins
Outdoor Recreation for 21st Century America
by H. Ken Cordell
Outdoor Recreation Management: Theory and Application, Third Edition
by Alan Jubenville and Ben Twight
Parks for Life: Moving the Goal Posts, Changing the Rules, and Expanding the Field
by Will LaPage
The Pivotal Role of Leisure Education: Finding Personal Fulfillment in This Century
edited by Elie Cohen-Gewerc and Robert A. Stebbins
Planning and Organizing Group Activities in Social Recreation
by John V. Valentine
Planning Areas and Facilities for Sport and Recreation: Predesign Process, Principles, and Strategies
by Jack A. Harper
Planning Parks for People, Second Edition
by John Hultsman, Richard L. Cottrell, and Wendy Z. Hultsman
Programming for Parks, Recreation, and Leisure Services: A Servant Leadership Approach, Third Edition
by Donald G. DeGraaf, Debra J. Jordan, and Kathy H. DeGraaf
Puttin' on the Skits: Plays for Adults in Managed Care
by Jean Vetter

Recreation and Leisure: Issues in an Era of Change, Third Edition
    edited by Thomas Goodale and Peter A. Witt
Recreation and Youth Development
    by Peter A. Witt and Linda L. Caldwell
Recreation for Older Adults: Individual and Group Activities
    by Judith A. Elliott and Jerold E. Elliott
Recreation Program Planning Manual for Older Adults
    by Karen Kindrachuk
Recreation Programming and Activities for Older Adults
    by Jerold E. Elliott and Judith A. Sorg-Elliott
Reference Manual for Writing Rehabilitation Therapy Treatment Plans
    by Penny Hogberg and Mary Johnson
Service Living: Building Community through Public Parks and Recreation
    by Doug Wellman, Dan Dustin, Karla Henderson, and Roger Moore
Simple Expressions: Creative and Therapeutic Arts for the Elderly in Long-Term Care Facilities
    by Vicki Parsons
A Social Psychology of Leisure
    by Roger C. Mannell and Douglas A. Kleiber
Special Events and Festivals: How to Organize, Plan, and Implement
    by Angie Prosser and Ashli Rutledge
Survey Research and Analysis: Applications in Parks, Recreation, and Human Dimensions
    by Jerry Vaske
Taking the Initiative: Activities to Enhance Effectiveness and Promote Fun
    by J. P. Witman
Therapeutic Recreation and the Nature of Disabilities
    by Kenneth E. Mobily and Richard D. MacNeil
Therapeutic Recreation: Cases and Exercises, Second Edition
    by Barbara C. Wilhite and M. Jean Keller
Therapeutic Recreation in Health Promotion and Rehabilitation
    by John Shank and Catherine Coyle
Therapeutic Recreation in the Nursing Home
    by Linda Buettner and Shelley L. Martin
Therapeutic Recreation Programming: Theory and Practice
    by Charles Sylvester, Judith E. Voelkl, and Gary D. Ellis
Therapeutic Recreation Protocol for Treatment of Substance Addictions
    by Rozanne W. Faulkner
The Therapeutic Recreation Stress Management Primer
    by Cynthia Mascott
The Therapeutic Value of Creative Writing
    by Paul M. Spicer
Traditions: Improving Quality of Life in Caregiving
    by Janelle Sellick
Trivia by the Dozen: Encouraging Interaction and Reminiscence in Managed Care
    by Jean Vetter